Frontispiece

When the Great War (World War One) broke out in 1914, many civilians and recruits imagined that the conflict would develop in a glamorous, colorful way at least as described in their poetry. Despite the realism of this poster's background and even late in the war, many shared this distorted view of the trench experience—but how could they express it accurately, given their education and values? (*Victoria Daily Times*, 13 September 1918, 13.)

THE ONES WHO

HAVE TO PAY

THE SOLDIER-POETS OF VICTORIA BC
IN THE GREAT WAR 1914-1918

ROBERT RATCLIFFE TAYLOR

Order this book online at www.trafford.com
or email orders@trafford.com

Most Trafford titles are also available at major online book retailers.

Printed in the United States of America.

ISBN: 978-1-4669-9034-0 (sc)
ISBN: 978-1-4669-9036-4 (hc)
ISBN: 978-1-4669-9035-7 (e)

Library of Congress Control Number: 2013907215

Trafford rev. 05/10/2013

 www.trafford.com

North America & international
toll-free: 1 888 232 4444 (USA & Canada)
phone: 250 383 6864 ♦ fax: 812 355 4082

C O N T E N T S

LIST OF ILLUSTRATIONS

Chapter III The Soldiers' Poems

Chapter IV The Soldiers' Lives

ACKNOWLEDGEMENTS

For their friendly assistance, I am indebted to the staff at the British Columbia Archives and the Oak Bay Archives in Victoria, the Microforms Room and the Special Collections of the Library of the University of Victoria, including Ryan Watson of the Technical Support Unit, and the Local History Room of the Library of Greater Victoria. Throughout my research and writing, my wife Anne provided constant support. Dr. Roberta M. Styran offered useful criticism and encouragement. Of course, any mistakes or misconceptions in this book are my own.

"The best poetry of the Great War is not necessarily typical;
the most useful historical evidence is often to be found in mere 'verse'."

Dominic Hubbard and John Onions (eds.),
Poetry of the Great War. An Anthology
(London: Macmillan, 1986), 2.

INTRODUCTION

Verse as Useful Historical Evidence

The First World War, or the "Great War", occurred a century ago. Much has been written about that cataclysmic event. Academic and popular histories still attract a large readership, and collections of diaries and letters readily find publishers on paper and on line. Many veterans wrote memoirs of their years in the trenches on the Western Front, works which still attract readers. In Canada, the magnificent performance of our soldiers at Vimy Ridge in 1917 is endlessly retold. Even in the twenty-first century, Canadian novelists such as Joseph Boyden in his *Three Day Road* [2005] and Canadian film-makers such as Paul Gross with his *Passchendaele* (2008) have added their interpretations.

As for this essay, it attempts to describe how young (and older) men from Victoria, British Columbia, in training there, or somehow connected to the city, experienced the "Great War".[1] I have chosen local servicemen's poetry as evidence of their response to the extraordinary circumstances in which they found themselves in the trenches. Their poems are windows into the minds of our Canadian great-grandparents—especially those living in Victoria BC a hundred years ago. Through their verse, we may learn to understand their motives and ideals and, by contrast and comparison, we learn more about ourselves today.

In September 1914, and even later in 1915, Victoria's citizens witnessed great scenes of enthusiasm as hundreds of men volunteered and left for training in Québec. [Fig.I.1] "We've buckled on our swords", exclaimed a local civilian poet in September 1914, and "we'll play them at their game." (*Victoria Daily Colonist*, 2 September, editorial page). We are "ready, aye, ready", wrote another in the same month (*Victoria Daily Times,* 12 September 1914, editorial page) The phenomenon was repeated across the country, of course, and in many ways Victoria's volunteers shared the aspirations and values of recruits from other parts of Canada. As I shall show, however, soldiers from Victoria and southern Vancouver Island had a slightly different mentality from those elsewhere. The letters and diaries of some of our servicemen written "on the spot" are available, of course, but my approach has been to collect and study the poetry which Victoria's soldiers sent home to local newspapers and journals (such as the *Victoria Daily Times* or *The Week*).

As well, I have studied the soldier's contributions to some of their regimental publications.[2] The latter contain regular infusions of poetry. For example, at the front, the Canadian Scottish published *The Brazier. A Trench Journal,* which often included "A Page of Poetry." Almost all contributions are by anonymous soldiers; only occasionally is the author's name given. Limericks were popular here as they were in *The Listening Post,* put out by the 7th Canadian Infantry Battalion (which included the 88th Victoria Fusiliers) in France. The 103rd Battalion supported *The Timber Wolf,* published at the armories in Victoria and later at the Willows Camp, also in that city. *The Western Scot* was published by the unit with the same name, first at "the Willows" and later at the front. Like *The Bantam Review*, published by the British Columbia Bantams at the Sidney Camp, north of Victoria, it regularly contained verse.

I chose to study Victoria's soldiers because, apart from the fact that I was born, raised and educated in British Columbia's capital, the city has rightly claimed to be substantially different from its sister, Vancouver, and indeed from many other Canadian cities of its size. In particular, the men of this community who volunteered in 1914 and later came from a milieu which was intensely British in its sympathies and relatively sophisticated in its culture, as I show in Chapter I.

William Wordsworth described poetry as "the spontaneous overflow of powerful feelings."[3] For most poets, whether amateur or "literary", writing verse is often an act of putting profound or moving experience into measured and structured form, thus making sense of and preserving it. The vast majority of Victoria's soldier-poets had no university education; hence they had not been exposed to poetry as an academic discipline. However, their experience of verse in public schools (dry and ritualized though it may have been) did not prevent them from writing poems themselves. On the other hand, the British journalist and veteran Charles Montague, who published influential memoirs in 1922, marveled that any of his countrymen in the trenches had any energy left over after performing their regular trench duties.[4] Most soldiers were indeed too exhausted often to write anything, much less poetry. "Powerful feelings", however, did compel some men to write. Faced with life-altering experiences, Victoria's soldiers—like thousands of others in the armed forces of all the belligerents—sought not only to describe them in letters and diaries but also to provide structure to those events which might give shape and meaning to them. Through its use of meter and rhyme, verse often seemed to them to be a better medium than prose.

Others have examined the poetry of servicemen of the Great War, most notably Paul Fussell whose *The Great War and Modern Memory* (1975) is a classic. However, his poets were mainly men with a literary education and aspirations to universal significance and moral profundity. My soldier-poets did not write great poetry. Some readers would label it mere "verse", but their poems have the virtue of sincerity and a desire to communicate. Unlike Victoria's civilian poets who remained afflicted with romantic illusions as to the reality of the war, the men in the trenches wrote "with the authority of direct experience".[5] A pre-war resident of Victoria, Robert Service, prefaced his wartime "Rhymes of a Red Cross Man" with the couplet,

> *So here's my sheaf of war-worn verse,*
> *And some is bad—and some is worse . . .*[6]

Service was too modest and, of course, my soldier-poets would be astonished to find their own "war-worn verse" the subject of a local historian's analysis. But, as I hope to show, their poetry, even if occasionally awkward and inept, offers a window into the minds and hearts of its composers.

None of the poems that I cite are "bad", in the sense that Service means; most of the submitted few that are "worse" I assume were not published and the few that were I have not used. To the argument that much of what newspaper editors chose to publish was propaganda for the Canadian government and military leaders, I counter that officially inspired messages always reflect views which are held by at least part of the target population. And so while these verses echo the attitudes of Victoria's opinion-making elites, they also document the views of the men who learned from them. (Not even the "big lie" falls on ground which is not already prepared in some way to receive it.) Furthermore, Daphne Read has correctly written that the verse of local poets has "an intimate connection to the oral traditions of the locale while fulfiling some of the function of the minstrels of a preliterate age."[7]

A famous British recruiting poster of the Great War shows a little girl sitting on her father's lap and a boy on the floor nearby playing with toy soldiers. The girl points to a page in a book and asks, "Daddy, what did *you* do in the Great War?" He looks uneasy because evidently he did not enlist to support the national cause. On the other hand, our younger generations might imagine themselves asking their great-grandfathers questions such as "*why* did you volunteer in 1914?"—not, of course to provoke embarrassment, but to understand their way of thinking, which may seem quite different from ours today.

To young people in the twenty-first century, the Great War may seem a futile, misguided, even ridiculous endeavor. And to a degree it was but, to most Victoria residents, it did not seem so at the time. This essay may answer younger readers' curiosity on this score, because the poetry offers a glimpse into the solders' minds as well as those of their sons, brothers, wives and lovers, who endured that great conflict a century ago.

Because of this, the soldiers' verse challenges us to examine our own attitudes today. It is as if we have approached a magnificent old house and are able to look through the windows into some of the rooms. The contents are fascinating; we marvel and we learn. Of course, our view is limited and we can't see the whole of the mansion's interior, but what we can take in is challenging, even unsettling.

What criteria did I use in selecting these poets and their works? In most cases, I chose poems by men who were residents of Victoria and southern Vancouver Island or who were in training in the area or worked here. Some of the soldier-poets whom I quote were not native to Victoria but were in recuperation here at one of the military hospitals, as at nearby Sidney or in the municipality of Esquimalt. One of the local militia groups, the 50th Gordon Highlanders of Canada, trained at the Willows Exhibition Grounds in Oak Bay, Victoria's eastern-most suburb, but men from outside the city were located here, too, and so some of their poetry is included. I assume that some poems were sent to local editors here to be published because their authors had colleagues, friends or family here. (In these cases I have made surmises which cannot always be proven). Some verses which were sent through the wire services were hard to attribute to a Victoria native. In such cases, I have tried to discover if the author had a particular connection to Victoria. I insert such poems if they seem to reflect attitudes widespread in the community and in the minds of its sons. It is possible that some poems were "borrowed" by soldiers who claimed them as their own work—or that editors incorrectly attributed certain verses to the men who submitted them. Nevertheless, such poems still reflect attitudes and values of many of Victoria's servicemen and are worth reading.

Occasionally I have quoted from Victoria's civilian war poets, in order to show the background from which the servicemen came, and from non-Victorian poets chosen by Victoria's editors for inclusion in the newspapers because these poets also reflected popular and/or encouraged attitudes learned in the city's schools and churches. Again, the volunteers reflect views which they learned in their youth and absorbed from the general culture.

Imagining the voice of a dead comrade, one of these servicemen wrote, "My day is done and my race is run, and I'm one who has to pay, . . ." (*Colonist*, 16 December 1916, editorial page). The purpose of my essay is to ask: What did these men who had "to pay" feel about the war they were fighting? Why did they volunteer in 1914 and later? What were their personal values? Were they ever disillusioned or "blue" in the trenches of the Western Front? To what extent did they enjoy combat? How did they regard the German enemy? And, faced with artillery bombardment, execrable living conditions, and the fear of death or maiming, what helped them to "carry on"? Granted, the poems do not answer fully or all the questions which we might want to ask our ancestors. For example, although we learn that imperial patriotism was a powerful motive for volunteering early in the war, other motives for joining up existed, such as peer pressure, the need for a job during an economic recession, and youthful desire for adventure. Scholarly studies, such as those of Desmond Morton, document these motives.

The poems present some surprises. Younger readers may be amazed at what may seem to be the apparently blind loyalty to the British Empire on the part of Victoria's youth. They may also be distressed at the relatively few displays of pride in Canada. They will discover that some of our popular generalizations about Canadian soldiers' Great War experience are not supported by the evidence in Victoria's soldier-poets' verse. Journalists who annually proclaim that the Battle of Vimy Ridge marked the "coming to maturity of Canada as a nation" may be disappointed to find so few references to that "milestone" in the poems by Victoria's servicemen. Military history buffs may wonder why the poets express so little regard for the "comradeship" and "camaraderie" of the trenches. This study, therefore, raises questions which further research must answer.

On the other hand, by indirection the soldier-poets teach us about twenty-first century Canada or, indeed, the English-speaking world. How have we changed since 1914? Do we still have the same attitude to "honor", "duty", etc.? Vilolent conflict, devastating to soldiers as much as to civilians, has not disappeared in contemporary "civilization". With Canada's renewed commitment to wars overseas, and the present "war on terror", moreover, this essay may serve as a tribute to Canadian servicemen, past, present and future.

Notes to INTRODUCTION

1   I have focused on the Western Front at its worst, but am aware of the existence of "cushy sectors" there, of the fact that the war was fought in other theatres, and that the experience of Canada's allies might be different from that of British and Canadian soldiers.

2   I offer the source of quotations from poems in the body of the text, as here. Other citations are given in these endnotes.

3   William Wordsworth, Preface *to Lyrical Ballads, with Pastoral and other Poems* (London: Longman, Hurst, Rees, and Orme, 1805, I), 22.

4   Charles E. Montague, *Disenchantment* (New York: Brentano's, 1922), 65.

5   Samuel Hynes, *A War Imagined. The First World War and English Culture* (London: Bodley Head, 1990), 158.

6   "Rhymes of a Red Cross Man", *Collected Poems* (London: Benn, 1960, 292).

7   Daphne Read (ed.), *The Great War and Canadian Society, An Oral History* (Toronto: New Hogtown, 1978), 14.

CHAPTER I

THE SOLDIERS' VICTORIA

66 "An inspiring scene" was enacted at Victoria's inner harbor on August 26, 1914, when were heard "the shouts and cheers of [an] immense crowd", gathered to bid farewell to hundreds of equally enthusiastic volunteers. The men boarded the Canadian Pacific steamship PRINCESS MARY, which would take them to Vancouver whence they would travel to the training camp at Valcartier, Québec, and on to the battlefields of the Great War. The *Daily Colonist* described how the 5th Regiment, consisting of artillery-men from the local militia, marched through the city to the wharf, accompanied by "the crackle of musketry, the skirl of the pipes, [and] rousing and appropriate airs by bands . . ." (27 August 1914, 1). Two days later, the PRINCESS SOPHIA left with five hundred volunteers from the 50th Regiment, Gordon Highlanders, and the 88th Fusiliers of Victoria. The "sight was overwhelmingly impressive" said the *Colonist*, as thousands of people lined both sides of the harbor and Premier Richard McBride joined in wishing the militiamen godspeed (29 August 1914, 1). [Fig.I.1]

Fig. I.1: Troops Leaving Victoria:

The PRINCESS MARY leaving Victoria harbor with another cohort of volunteers, 14 February 1915. The enthusiasm of both civilians and soldiers is evident. (Image Courtesy of BC Archives Collections: C-08346)

Departing on these ships were several of the local poets whom I quote in this essay. Major Lorne Ross, for example, was one of the leaders of the 50th Regiment and Captain Robert Harvey was a member of the 88th Fusiliers. In later years, volunteers included the soldier-poets Charles Armstrong, Edward Vaughan, and Leonard McLeod Gould. Two of these men (Armstrong and Macleod) were former journalists. Most local soldier-poets, however, were not professionally trained in the use of the English language but had benefited from a good public school education and had been raised in a social climate which valued poetry. Part of the most literate generation in Canadian history, they all seem to have departed Victoria with the same enthusiasm as was expressed on the causeway, the grounds of the nearby Empress Hotel and the harbor wharves in 1914 and 1915. In their poetry can be heard the echoes of the fife and drum band and the cheers of those Victoria citizens who gave them such a spirited send-off in those fateful years.

A Literate Population

Many of those relatives, friends and supporters gathered at the harbor in the early years of the Great War enjoyed reading. In fact, nineteenth century Victoria was already a highly literate place. The settlement was founded in 1843 and by 1858 several newspapers served the community. As early as the latter year, Thomas Hibben had established a stationery and bookstore, and in 1864 David Spencer opened his own reading room and bookstore. Some early residents, such as Benjamin William Pearse, surveyor-general of the Colony of Vancouver Island, owned large libraries. Walter Colquhoun Grant, another early surveyor, arrived in 1849 with his large personal book collection. By the 1880s, Victoria had seen the establishment of a Shakespeare Club and the Alexandra Club for the enjoyment of music, art, and literature.

From the city's beginnings, education and its product, literacy, were important to local residents. On the outskirts of the city, Craigflower School, considered the first Canadian school built west of the Great Lakes, was founded in 1854. In 1860, the Girls' Collegiate School was established by the Anglican authorities. In 1886, the Provincial Museum was opened. In 1891 the Public (Carnegie) Library was established and, when Victoria College was founded in 1902, a campaign to have a local university was inaugurated. In 1911, construction began on a new four-storey high school, which became one of the most imposing structures in the community. In 1914, the Normal School for the training of teachers opened in an impressive towered structure on a rise overlooking the city.

Poetry in Victoria in 1914

"If you published a book of poems in London a hundred years ago, you could live for three years on the proceeds," avers a twenty-first century Victoria poet.[1] Many of our great-grandfathers and—grandmothers loved poetry. Canada was "a society in which poetry mattered", writes Jonathan Vance; "no other mode of public expression drew such a wide range of practitioners".[2] Indicative of the popularity of verse is the frequency with which it was published even in Victoria's labor union periodical, the *Semi-Weekly Tribune. A Journal of Industrial and Social Reconstruction.* Its editors—although committed to practical reform—expressed their enjoyment of poetry, traditional as well as polemical, offering several poems in every edition. In Victoria's more widely circulated dailies, the *Times* and the *Colonist,* the verse of poets employed as book-keepers, bureaucrats and glassblowers, for example, was published. Most of the soldier-poets were from this middle class, a relatively large group even in 1914. Although some heavy industry had developed on its harbor shores, the city was predominantly a bourgeois place, with a large literate population of provincial government employees, professionals, white collar workers, craftsmen, men from the new skilled trades, and already (by 1900) many well-educated retirees.

A century ago, the writing and the enjoyment of poetry was not the preserve of an elite of "intellectual" or "academic" writers remote from the general public. The ability to conjure up a verse to be read aloud at a social occasion or important public event was considered a normal accomplishment of a man or woman of almost any social class. In newspapers, journals, magazines and pamphlets, political rhymes were disseminated for popular reading. Advertisers used poetry to hawk their products. For a long time before and after 1914, classic poems had to be memorized in school, a procedure which, however dreary, nevertheless imbued a sense of rhythm, rhyme and imagery in many a child. Reaching adulthood, even if individuals never wrote any verse, they were receptive to the poems which they read in local journals.

In Canada, therefore, public interest in reading and writing poetry seems to have peaked in the early years of the last century and, as I have indicated, not only among the better educated classes. The great increase in literacy in the late nineteenth century, due to the expansion of compulsory primary education, meant that a large group of literate readers and listeners existed. As well, Mechanics' Institutes and public libraries had infused a respect for literature among the general public which has never since been equaled. Of course, an upper class education (which included the Greek and Latin classics) would help the reader to appreciate some of the more arcane published verse with its references to the legends, history and literature of the ancient world.

With the development of typesetting machines and high-speed steam-powered presses, the production of daily and weekly newspapers was becoming mechanized. In Canada, between Confederation (1867) and the outbreak of the Great War (1914), newspaper circulation increased over three times. In these publications, hometown readers read local poets with special pleasure because they expressed what was on many residents' minds. Even when the writers were not local persons, newspaper editors printed their poems when they thought the sentiment expressed therein was relevant to the home town community and its attitudes, values, and problems.

From their inception in 1858 and 1884, respectively, the *Colonist* and the *Times* regularly published poetry by locals and non-residents as well as by the well-known British, American and Canadian writers. Verse was also published regularly by such local periodicals as *The Week* and the aforementioned *Semi-Weekly Tribune.* As early as 1864, the *Colonist*—or the *British Colonist,* as it was then known—allotted a long column on page three to verse—and this in editions which usually ran to only four pages in total! On 5 June 1884, the *Colonist* announced a policy of promoting local poets' works. Poems were even occasionally featured on the front page of the two main dailies. Inside, often two or three poems would appear in one edition. Those printed on the editorial page expressed the opinion of the editors. Significant poems were published inside a frame, drawing attention to their themes.

The local newspapers also occasionally published articles about poetry. The *Colonist,* for example, offered detailed comment on Canada's Charles G.D. Roberts in 1907 and on Rudyard Kipling in 1908. Before the Great War, the themes of published verse in Victoria were similar to those across the English-speaking world of the nineteenth century: love, death, children, religious faith, nature, landscape, humor, and politics. Poems for children and for women were frequent. Both the *Times* and the *Colonist* published the equivalent of a "poem of the day".

Charles Swayne, who began employment at the *Colonist* in 1909 and became editor-in-chief in 1917, had a particular interest in literature and the arts, a fact which may account for the greater prevalence of poetry in that newspaper, compared to the *Times.* Assuming that its readers were familiar with Shakespeare, the

Colonist could use passages from his works to satirize current provincial politics. This practice began even before Swayne's time. Taking a dig at local politics, for example, the newspaper's editors used a passage from "The Merchant of Venice" on 4 March 1867. The *Colonist* also reproduced the "Prologues" written in blank verse for private amateur theatrical performances (11 October 1871 and 14 August 1881). Poems written to commemorate events important to part of the local community, such as the retirement of a popular clergyman, were published (*Colonist,* 29 June 1887). Important here is the fact that, as the Great War developed, the *Vancouver Sun* published only five poems in September 1914, whereas the *Colonist*—in contrast—printed fifty-three in that month, and the *Times,* twenty-nine.

The *Colonist* tended to support the policies of the Conservative Party, while the *Times* favored the Liberals. In choosing verse for publication, however, the editors of both Victoria's main newspapers agreed with the views of the political, professional and literary elite of Victoria and of Canada, particularly during a time of national crisis. That elite included clergymen and school teachers who—before, during and after the war—instilled their tastes and values in young people, most of whom, by 1900, spent at least six or seven years in the public school and Sunday School systems. And so, evidence from these periodicals and from other sources (letters, diaries, and secondary studies) suggests that editors reflected rather than formed current views about art, politics, and war. Thus the absence of local criticism of Canada's entry into the Great War grew out of Victoria's traditions. Most of its citizens (at every class level and profession) were ready in 1914 to support a European war for the British Empire's sake and to encourage their young men to volunteer to serve. A different situation prevailed in prairie cities, where Central European immigration was a factor, and in Québec, where potentially anti-British feeling could erupt. Pacifism was not unknown in British Columbia but its adherents remained without much influence.

To be sure, a degree of control over the print media—and some resistance to directives—existed in Victoria. During the war years, local editors, following the urgings of Ottawa's Chief Press Censor, Ernest J. Chambers, hoped that well-chosen poems might reinforce pre-existent attitudes to military service or the British connection. When Chambers sent memoranda to newspaper editors, indicating what he considered unsuitable for publication, editors usually complied. If periodicals that were usually supportive strayed from the government line, they were reprimanded gently, but a journal such as Victoria's *The Week,* which became socialist and pacifist in tone was actually shut down in 1918. During the first year of the war, the *Times* was more adventurous than the *Colonist,* perhaps because it had long been in sympathy with the federal Liberal party (now out of office) and hence was less inclined to support the policies of the Conservative government of Sir Robert Borden, who was in power in 1914. The *Times* occasionally published verse which could be considered more realistic, even possibly critical, vis-à-vis the war. Ultimately, however, censorship put an end to such daring. Later, when a poem might be considered less than "uplifting", both dailies tended to "bury" it on their back pages; i.e. not on page four, the editorial page, but on, for example, page seventeen.

Did Victoria's editorial offices ever receive a poem from a soldier deeply critical of the war effort or shockingly despondent over his experiences? We shall probably never know. The editors self-censored because they did not want to lose touch with sources of news. They lacked the self-confidence of a later generation of newspapermen who demanded to know more than they were officially told. To be fair, they could not know that some photographs sent from Europe might be fabricated—as was occasionally the case during the tenure of Max Aitken as director of the Canadian War Records Office in England.

If Victoria's editors ever questioned the purpose of, or were disillusioned with, the nature of the Great War, they saw their role as encouraging optimism and maintaining public morale. When the Germans threatened to break through the Allied lines in their great offensive beginning on 21 March 1918, the *Times* editors, perhaps inspired by a spontaneous influx of local morale-boasting verse, launched their own offensive. Although they had published no poetry at all in the previous five weeks, on 30 March they printed "Never Despair" (6) and followed it with five poems containing "uplifting" themes, such as "Look for the Bits of Blue" (25 April, 6) in the next month.

In the first years of the war at least, the editors of both the *Times* and the *Colonist* saw to it that verse continued to be published regularly as a form of comfort in those difficult times. For example, the *Times* published an occasional feature on its editorial page, "Passages from the Poets", including works by Robert Browning, Lord Tennyson, and Robert Burns. By 1918, however, the frequency of published poetry declined. In the case of the *Colonist,* for example, two regular features which consistently contained verse were discontinued. In the *Times'* case, the featured "poem of the day" (often a British or American classic) ceased in September 1915. The number of poems published on the editorial pages also declined in 1917-1918. Not unexpectedly, the year 1919 saw an increase in "In Memoriam" poetry in both newspapers, which commemorated local men killed in action.

The reasons for the decline of published verse in the war years are hard to discern. Certainly, lists of casualties took up space, often on the editorial pages. Possibly some editors had come to doubt that verse could have a salutary effect on public morale. Perhaps the inflated diction of wartime verse had come to seem tedious—even duplicitous—to editors, poets and readers. Conceivably Victoria's soldier poets had become too exhausted by stress to compose and submit verse, a situation which could apply to civilian writers, too. As well, technological developments meant that by at least 1919 more photographs were being published, which took up space formerly allocated to features such as verse.

A Hurricane of Poetry

Canadian soldiers of the Great War wrote and enjoyed much poetry—and they often wrote confidently. While serving with the Canadian Expeditionary Force, Sergeant William W. Murray sent one of his poems to Rudyard Kipling, who graciously replied.[3] Lieutenant-Colonel Cyrus Peck of Prince Rupert, BC, who volunteered in Victoria in 1914, and was later in command the 16th Battalion, "charmed the officers' mess with recitations from Shelley and Keats, poets Peck revered . . . ."[4] Among the lower ranks, poetry was read and recited. Robert Service's work was popular with many. Victoria's George Jarvis carried "'Songs of a Sourdough' with him into the trenches."[5] In the hours before an attack, Paymaster F.C. Bagshaw and Saskatchewan volunteer Dave McCabe, for example, recited Robert Burns and Shakespeare to each other.[6] This love of verse continued after the war. For example, Lieutenant-Colonel George C. Machum included five of his own poems in his *Story of the 64th Battalion, C.E.F. 1915-1916.* Every one of the chapters of R.C. Fetherstonhaugh's *The Royal*

Montreal Regiment, 14ᵗʰ Battalion, C.E.F. 1914-1935 begins with a quotation of poetry. Lieutenant Ralph Lewis of the 25ᵗʰ Battalion quotes Kipling in his memoirs.[7] Few of these men were "English majors" at university—if, indeed, they had had any post-secondary education. The works of Victoria's soldier-poets, however, show a similar familiarity with the poetry of both classic and modern writers, such as Thomas Gray and Lewis Carroll.

Perhaps inevitably, in the hands of some of these often young soldiers, desperate for distraction and amusement, the canon of English verse was not safe from parody. The "Elegy Written in a Country Church-Yard" composed by Thomas Gray in 1750, which many a soldier had had to memorize in school, was lampooned by one "R.A.L.", "a Victoria boy". At least one of Gray's verses is still relatively well-known:

> *The boast of heraldry, the pomp of power,*
> > *And all that beauty, all that wealth e'er gave,*
> *Awaits alike th' inevitable hour:—*
> > *The paths of glory lead but to the grave.*

"R.A.L." neatly skewered its bombast with:

> *The boast of ribbons, nor the pomp of spurs,*
> > *Nor all the stripes of which a man could think,*
> *Can keep canteens open after hours.*
> > *The paths of pleasure lead but to the clink.*

(*Colonist*, 23 June 1917, editorial page)

Perhaps between these lines is the soldier's sense that the high-minded rhetoric of the original—which he had been taught to admire in school—had little relevance in the twentieth-century and certainly not in the trenches. Such parodies, however, indicate that Victoria's soldier-poets had a knowledge of classical poetry. Some were familiar with popular verse as well. In his "The Face at Courcelette", Kenneth George Halley of Ganges, north of Victoria, seems to have known some of the early works of Robert Service, for the following lines have the rhythm of the latter's verse:

> Tho' many nights show their fearful sights, still there's one
>   I can't forget
> —It's the moonlit space and the still dead face of the man at
>   Courcelette.

(Colonist, 16 December 1916, editorial page)

"Almost simultaneously with the Great War has come a renaissance of Poetry", wrote an editor of a Canadian verse anthology in 1916.[8] Perhaps naturally, men who had written a few stanzas before 1914 expressed their reaction to military service in verse. Moreover, many of the first to volunteer and for whom the war had most meaning (at least initially) were the most idealistic, sensitive, intelligent and better educated of the younger generation. In the Great War, thousands of this literate cohort regularly wrote letters home (much censored) and war diaries (secretly because usually forbidden), as well as verse, some of which was intended for publication.

As the war continued, more and more poems came from soldiers serving in the British—which at first included the Canadian—armies, so many that eventually the *Westminster Gazette* had to declare a moratorium on poems from the front. The *Wipers* [Ypres] *Times* (a British army newspaper published on the front line from February 1916 to the end of the war) commented wryly on the "hurricane of poetry," that was sweeping the British forces.[9] Of course, much of the poetry which I quote is derivative in style and none achieved the impact, in theme, of the works of such British war poets as Wilfred Owen, Siegfried Sassoon, Robert Graves, or Isaac Rosenberg. But as a record of deeply felt experience, each poem serves as a historical document of a local man's response to a national catastrophe and offers insight into the mindset of Victoria's citizens a hundred years ago.

Overseas Englishmen

Many Victoria residents had a powerful sense of their "Britishness", particularly their "Englishness". [Fig. I.2] Probably nowhere else in Canada did British imperial pride flourish as it did in Victoria. This profound sense of ethnic identity was a quality noted by visitors and assiduously cultivated by some locals. In fact, many Victoria people regarded themselves not so much as Canadians as "overseas Englishmen or—women",[10] essentially British people transplanted to a pleasant exile. For the traveler, John Foster Fraser, writing in 1911, the city embodied "a refined English society".[11] He would have noticed how various organizations, such as the "Sons of England" (founded 1874), reflected Victoria's attachment to "the old country". By 1900, branches of the British Navy League and the British Empire League were operating in Victoria. In 1913 the Imperial Order of the Daughters of the Empire established a branch here.

Although the original population of the colony included people of several different ethnic backgrounds, a cohort of the British "imperial" element soon arrived and dominated.[12] They came often from the colonies in south and east Asia, settling in Victoria because of its special ambience ("a little bit of olde England" as the

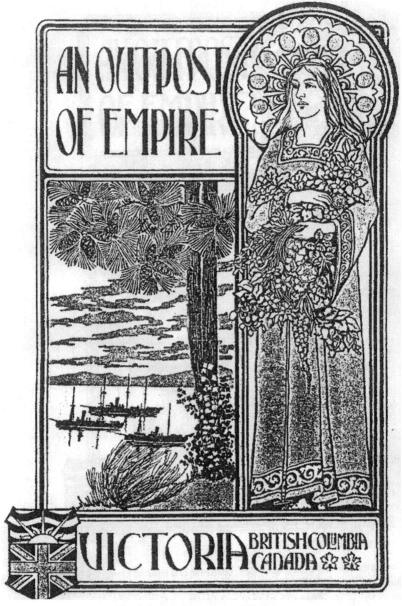

Fig.I.2: An Outpost of Empire

A 1904 appeal to tourists stressed Victoria's role in "the chain of Empire" and the presence of the nearby Esquimalt naval base, defending Britain's imperial interests. The allegorical figure suggested the bounties of nature in the area. (Victoria Tourist Association pamphlet cover, 1904.)

later tourist brochures maintained) and its mild climate, not as rainy and cold as the British Isles, yet not as hot and humid as parts of Asia or Africa. Even before the opening of the Panama Canal in 1913, the nearness of the Pacific Ocean provided a link to Britain's Asian empire. By the 1890s, the Canadian Pacific Railway's liners had begun regular sailings to Asia and Victoria became became a port of call for the EMPRESS OF RUSSIA and the EMPRESS OF ASIA on this "All Red Route". The completion of the Canadian Pacific Railway to the west coast in 1886 and the establishment of regular steamship connections across the Strait of Georgia cemented links to the rest of Canada. Tourists from North America and from Europe began to appear regularly. On the inner harbor, the significantly named Empress Hotel opened in 1908. Between 1886 and 1914 occurred the "Great Migration" of immigrants directly from the United Kingdom. By 1901, the Canadian census recorded that one third of the population of Victoria identified themselves as British-born (7,273 out of 23,688), a figure which would not include those born in Victoria of British immigrant parents and with relatives still resident in the "old country".[13] Now, as writers and journalists could travel to Vancouver Island more easily, imperialist poets such as Bliss Carman and Rudyard Kipling visited the city. Carman sensed a "British" quality in Victoria, calling it "a gracious imperial city".[14]

Many local citizens would have agreed. Clive Phillips-Wolley, British-born but long resident in the Victoria area, wrote a poem quoted in the *Colonist* on its front page, 18 August 1907, urging the "clasping of the hands" of people of British background all over the world;

Hands that as hands of children
Clasped round one mother's knee.
The old, old love they look back to;
The country over the sea.

For many residents of Victoria, Britain was the "Mother Country", an image developed in both poetry and graphic art. A wartime appeal from the British Red Cross showed a helmeted Britannia carrying a wounded soldier, with "Canada" in a nurse's cap declaring, "Let me help you carry the burden, Mother" (*Colonist* 14 October 1917, 16). "Mother has called", W. E. Peirce reminded the 88th Battalion in 1917 (*Times*, 10 June, 7).

Typically on 7 March 1887, the *Colonist* had published on its editorial page an anonymous poem which declared that the Union Jack was "the only flag for Canada": the writer did not want any version of the Canadian Red Ensign. Events which symbolized the city's connection to Great Britain were celebrated as when the Duke and Duchess of Cornwall and York visited Victoria in 1901: welcoming arches were constructed, bells were rung and cannons boomed. Milestones in the lives of the British royal family were honored here, because the English monarch was, then as now, the constitutional head of Canada: in 1911, for example, on King Edward VII's death, Victoria's streetcars were draped in purple and black. "My ancestors were Englishmen, an Englishman am I," declared a Member of the Legislative Assembly at a local St. George's Day dinner in Victoria in 1888; "and 'tis my boast that I was born "Beneath a British sky" (*Colonist,* 27 April, 2). Victoria, as "Britannia's far-flung battle line", had a special role to play in the Empire, wrote one poet in 1906—protecting "Yukon's oil and gold" (*Colonist,* 21 November, editorial page) and serving British interests. Of *British* Columbia [my emphasis], one poet wrote,

British institutions make
  Her wealth of products worth
A hundred fold for Britain's sake,
  Whose banner belts the earth.

(*Colonist,* 1 December 1877, 2)

In the 1890s, the *Colonist* carried "News from London" and "Late London Gossip" on its front pages. This sense of "Britishness" did not wane in the early twentieth century. When the South African (or Boer) War (1899-1902) erupted, the outpouring of imperialist, militarist, and patriotic verse in Victoria's newspapers prefigured that of 1914.

The loyalty of such "overseas Englishmen" was not merely to the Britain itself but to its overseas imperium as well. As late as 1945, when my age cohort started school in Victoria, we were still being shown the proud expanse of red (or pink) spread over maps of the globe documenting the ostensibly admirable extent of the "empire upon which the sun never sets". "Empire Day"—May 24—involved patriotic marches of school children. In my case, we were assembled on the steps of the Legislative Buildings in Victoria to sing "Land of Hope and Glory"—the land in question was Great Britain, not Canada. Not surprisingly, therefore, such pedagogy had even more influence in the first two decades of the twentieth century, when even the Commonwealth was still in its infancy. The British Empire was said to offer its subjects not only "hope and glory" (as the anthem asserted) but also liberty. In 1902, for example, when the Pacific cable was completed, W. J. Dowler, Victoria's City Clerk, praised "Britannia", as the "noblest Fount of Liberty divine" (*Colonist,* 1 November 1902, 4). During the Great War, teachers were encouraged to stress the justice of Canada's cause and the rightness of all things British. This attitude was exemplified in J. McMaster's poem in the *Times* on 11 February 1916 (editorial page), which began "O, Britain, mother of the world : . . ."

Given these declarations of loyalty to Britain, and particularly to England, my readers will not be surprised to find poets exulting in the vast extent and sheer power of the British Empire, of which Victoria was an integral part. In his "The Song of the Cities", which included Bombay and Singapore, Kipling had extolled the city in

VICTORIA

From East to West the circling world was passed,
Till West is East beside our land-locked blue;
From East to West the tested chain holds fast,
The well-forged link holds true!"[15]

Later in the *Colonist* (21 July, 1910), Phillips-Wolley declared, "British are we," meaning Canada, and Victoria in particular. He predicted correctly that:

When Britain's foemen meet,
We will not question if She's wrong or right—
At the first flap of that old flag—we fight.

His poem was published on the daily's editorial page. Needless to say, such sentiments were popular in Victoria. This kind of poem, said a writer in the *Times,* "set all the pulses of the Empire beating the faster in unison" (2 May 1908, 51).

Victoria commemorated Britain's past military victories. The centenary of the Battle of Trafalgar, for example, was celebrated lustily in 1905. In that year, looking ahead to a future great conflict involving Canada and the Empire, Phillips-Wolley was unconcerned, declaring,

> *This may be our Armageddon; seas may purple with*
> *blood and flame . . .*
> *What matter? There have been none like us, nor any to*
> *tame our pride . . .*[16]

F. Mortimer Kelley, another Victoria writer, also anticipated war with enthusiasm. "'Round about the old world sweeps a roar of coming strife," he declared in 1899; "all the anvils, loudly ringing, sound the glories of the sword" (*Colonist,* 4 May 1899, 2). About 1910, the Vancouver poet, Tom MacInnes, found himself on Victoria's Beacon Hill and wrote "Prone on a grassy knoll where runs the sea" In from the North Pacific, deep and blue," exulting in the "magnificent advance" of the British Empire. He would

> *Cry contempt upon that sickly creed*
> *That would not fire a shot to save its own . . .*
> *. . . Nay, rather let us guard*
> *The barest rock that flies our flag at all hazard.*

It was "naked truth" "that when a people lose the power to kill" They count for naught among the sons of men . . ."; "Then give us rifles—rifles everywhere—" "Ready rifles, tipt with bayonets!"[17]

Ernest McGaffey, an American-born Victoria poet and travel writer, published an imperialist ode on the editorial page of the *Colonist,* 4 February 1914. He reversed an accepted truism:

> *There is no need for British men*
> *To ever bend the knee:*
> *The sword is mightier than the pen*
> *While Britain rules the sea.*

Dr. Albert Watson, like so many poets—and their journalists and their readers—associated the British Empire with "freedom", although how they defined that term is unclear. In a poem entitled "Victoria", published on the editorial page of the *Times* (19 August 1910), Watson eulogized the city, with its naval base, as a "guardian":

> *I hear Esquimalt's thunder*
>   *Go booming down the breeze.*
> *The righteous will of freedom still*
>   *Be sovereign of the seas.*

Obviously, the prospect of military conflict was exciting to many local residents and poets. When war in South Africa threatened, an anonymous poet featured on the editorial page of the *Times* (17 October 1899) welcomed it, declaring, "We long to hear cannons roar . . .". The desired conflict broke out in the year of his poem, when the South African Boers refused to accept the "liberty" of the British Empire. Victoria expressed more enthusiasm for the war than did any other part of Canada. When war erupted again in the summer of 1914, thousands of British Columbians flocked to enlist in BC's capital, in Vancouver or in Valcartier, Québec. In Victoria, people again expressed enthusiasm, optimism about certain victory, and joy at the prospect of their men participating in military conflict far away. For them, the southern tip of Vancouver Island was a part of "Great" Britain whose interests anywhere in the world were theirs also. And so, as in 1899-1902, they expressed their loyalty and commitment in verse and sent off their willing sons and husbands to defend the Empire overseas.

Notes to THE SOLDIERS' VICTORIA

1   "Today if you publish a book of poems you can live for a week." A poet quoted by Sara Cassidy, in "Shift. The State of Storytelling", *Focus* (Victoria, BC), June 2007, 34.

2   In particular, he continues, "poetry was the primary literary form where the memory of the Great War was negotiated and expressed" ["Battle Verse. Poetry and Nationalism After Vimy Ridge", in Geoffrey Hayes, Andre Iarocci, and Mike Bechthold (eds.), *Vimy Ridge. A Canadian Reassessment,* (Waterloo, Ont,: Wilfrid Laurier University Press, 2007), 266].

3   W.W. Murray ("The Orderly Sergeant"), *Five Nines and Whizbangs* (Ottawa: Perrault (The Legionary Library), 1937), 113-114.

4   Mark Zuehlke, *Brave Battalion. The Remarkable Saga of the 16th Battalion (Canadian Scottish) in the First World War* (Mississauga: Wiley, 2008), 148.

5   Muriel Jarvis Ackinclos, *For the Love of George. In Old Victoria and World War One* (Victoria: First Choice, 2005), 79.

6   Ted Barris, *Victory at Vimy. Canada Comes of Age, April 9-12, 1917* (Toronto: Thomas Allen, 2007), 87.

7   Ralph Lewis, *Over the Top with the 25th Battalion. Chronicle of Events at Vimy Ridge and Courcelette* (Halifax: Marshall, 1918), 6.

8   John W. Garvin (ed.), *Canadian Poets of the Great War* (Toronto: McClelland, Goodchild and Stewart, 1916), 5.

9   Quoted in Samuel Hynes, *A War Imagined. The First World War and English Culture* (London: Bodley Head, 1990), 189.

10 Sandra Gwyn, *Tapestry of War. A Private View of Canadians in the Great War* (Toronto: Harper Collins, 1992), 74.

11 John F. Fraser, *Canada As It Is* (London: Cassell, 1911), 193.

12 Two recent books by John F. Bosher have developed this point in detail: *Imperial Vancouver Island. Who Was Who, 1850-1950* (Xlibris, 2010), and *Vancouver Island in the Empire* (Llumina, 2012).

13 *Fourth Census of Canada 1901* (Ottawa: King's Printer, 1902, I), 16.

14 Bliss Carman, *Poems* (New York: Dodd, Mead, 1931) 489.

15 Rudyard Kipling, *Collected Verse* (London: Hodder & Stoughton, 1912), 91.

16 Clive Phillips-Wolley, *Songs from a Young Man's Land* (Toronto: Thomas Allen, 1917), 37.

17 Tom MacInnes, *In Amber Lands: Poems* (New York: Broadway, 1910), 124-127.

CHAPTER II

THE SOLDIERS' WAR EXPERIENCE

1 Launcelot versus Krupp

For decades now, historians have marveled at the illusions about modern warfare held by the recruits of 1914. As well, they have noted the romantic language with which the volunteers anticipated and described (until late in the war) their military experience. Victoria's soldier-poets were no different. In recounting this phenomenon, I have tried to avoid condescension as much as a melodramatic style because our great-grandfathers were products of their education and their culture. Inevitably, however, when describing their Great War experience, they used vocabulary and imagery which gave a false impression of the events in France and Flanders.

Language That is Unfamiliar Today [1]

Victoria's soldier-poets were raised on the romantic poetry and novels of the nineteenth century. In these works, war and the soldier's life was presented as adventurous and glamorous.

Individual heroic deeds were possible. Military conflict was akin to strenuous outdoor exercise, dangerous but invigorating. Accordingly, many of our poets anticipated service in Europe as a colorful sporting event. When a poet had experienced astonishing and horrifying events in the trenches, however, he struggled to find the words to express what he saw and felt—and usually failed. The English language was simply inadequate to express the feelings and reactions of the twentieth century soldier in a conflict unprecedented in its mass miseries. And so, because poets were familiar only with traditional verse, they tended to use the timeworn phrases and images of those poems. But the vocabulary and word pictures of the works of Tennyson or Macaulay, for example, had not preparer the volunteers of 1914 for the reality of powerful artillery barrages, gas attacks, machinegun fire and the desolation of "no-man's-land". Nor could these words and images adequately describe the soldier's response to them. And yet they were all that were available to the Victoria soldier-poet and so were what he used.

In 1914 the British literary scholar, Gilbert Murray, wrote hopefully that "the language of romance and melodrama has now become true."[2] We shall see, therefore, that Victoria's soldier-poets used words which described military conflict in a pre-industrial society, even before the invention of gunpowder. The enemy soldiers were the "foemen", who had amassed in "hosts". The result was a "fray". The pronouns "thee" and "thou" were used as in the Bible or Shakespeare.[3] The impression on the reader is that the European war would be a conflict between medieval armies in an agrarian society. For many of these men, especially before they experienced combat, warfare was anticipated to be, in Pierre Berton's words, "men in brilliant costumes galloping about on splendid horses."[4] They imagined that they would fight in a single campaign on an open field with cavalry charges, glittering sabers, and trumpets sounding. By December 1914 they would have seized Berlin. They conjured up images of flags and banners fluttering in the wind, as on an imagined medieval battlefield—and yet the fighting would be more chivalrous than ever took place in the nasty scrums of earlier centuries. [Fig. II.1.1]

The most vivid of these mis-imaginings is a 1914 poem by Lieutenant-Colonel W. Beale of Cadboro Bay (now a Victoria suburb), "The Lay of Liège", in which he claimed to describe the fierce resistance which that Belgian city put up to the German invasion. Beale suggested that European society had not changed since the middle ages, but remained in a rural idyll. His poem was a "lay", a medieval narrative song. Soldiers were "warriors"; trumpets were sounded and standards, unfurled; "horsemen and footmen" rallied; "serried hosts advance[d]". In the future, Beale predicted that when "the good man [a farmer] mends his ploughshare "And cleans his pruning hook" "When the good wife plies her needle", the "lay" of Liège will be recounted "with weeping and with laughter" (*Colonist,* 30 September 1914, 13). Similarly, "from furthest East to furthest West," wrote "G.M.D" (probably a civilian) in 1915, "we've heard the bugle's call", evoking memories of a boyhood reading of the saga of Roland and Charlemagne (*Colonist,* 28 March 1915, editorial page). Apart from the fact that these images were often historically inaccurate, they deluded both soldiers and civilian readers as to the real nature of the Great War.

Fig.II.1.1: "The Call"

The Canadian provinces "gird the loins" of the Canadian knight. Born in India, John Byam Liston Shaw (1872-1919) was a British artist specializing in imperial themes and a member of the "Artist Rifles", a regiment of British volunteers. Even in the year of Canada's conscription crisis, the authorities continued to use such imagery. (*Canada in Khaki*, Vol. I, 1917, opp. 4.)

Persistence of the Use of High Diction

Despite the intrusion of reality and experience, however, the high-flown rhetoric noticeable at the war's beginning survived. A local soldier-poet, Edward M.B. Vaughan, continued to write in the florid vein even while in France with Victoria's 88th Fusiliers. Some of his poetry is humorous but his "The First C.E.F." [Canadian Expeditionary Force], written a few weeks before his death in action in May 1917, revels in verbiage about "crimson banners" and "deathless heroes" (*Times*, 4 August 1917, 7).

On the other hand, some local soldier-poets who wrote about military service in the traditional mode found their poetic inspiration sapped over time by actual warfare, with the result that they wrote little about their experiences once they arrived in Europe. A very few actually downplayed the putative glamor of war and deliberately undercut the romantic image of, for example, the fearless Canadian warrior. "Don't make us one of the heroes, the johnnies the sages sing", wrote a local poet, Ralph Sheldon-Williams, reflecting a feeling among some Canadian soldiers that the concept of "hero" had become meaningless in the twentieth century.[5]

However, more typical was Charles L. Armstrong. A prolific Victoria poet before the war, upon enlistment in October 1915 he published several war-related poems and later (in 1916) when he was training with the Western Scots. The latter verse is more down-to-earth than much else that was published in Victoria at that time, but still bears little relationship to actual trench warfare. Although he reported on the Scots' experience in France in a prose article in the *Colonist* in November 1916, he published few poems while in service there. As Paul Fussell suggests, Armstrong probably did not possess the vocabulary precisely and realistically to describe his experiences, or, as Jay Winter writes, he became one of those "soldier-poets [who] could not stomach . . . the loftier versions of civilian romance about war".[6] Armstrong's poem "The Fallen Bell" is gloomy in tone. [Fig. II.9.1] It may be significant that, before the war ended, Armstrong was invalided home to Victoria with "heart trouble".

Few of the city's soldier-poets found a vocabulary that was less inflated and more realistic than Armstrong's. None wrote as bitterly or as angrily as Wilfred Owen or Siegfried Sassoon in England. No poems published in Victoria's periodicals and newspapers approached the devastating critique of Owen who, in his "Anthem for Doomed Youth", asked "What passing bells for those who die as cattle?" and who condemned the patriarchs who "slew . . . half the seed of Europe, one by one . . .". Of course, even Owen's works were first published privately in England in 1918 and only gradually became known to the reading public.

A Tropical Growth of Illusion

In Robert Service's book of war poems, "Rhymes of a Red Cross Man", the poet imagines one volunteer singing, "Oh, we're booked for the Great Adventure now, We're pledged to the Real Romance . . .".[7] The British journalist Charles Montague called such misconceptions about warfare which plagued his fellow volunteers in 1914 "a tropical growth of illusion".[8] The first poems published in Victoria by soldiers are similarly filled with enthusiasm over enlistment, the notion of going off on a "great adventure". In the fall of 1914, a cheerful, naïve fatalism colored some poets' outlook. B. De M. Andrew of the 88th Fusiliers expressed what many young men felt—and wanted others to feel—in a poem published on the editorial page of the *Colonist*, 22 November 1914. In part, it reads,

A Victorian's Ode

Don't think of death with fright;
Old Fate, with smirking glee,
Hath spun her nickel bright.

She hides the coin from sight;
It ain't for you and me
To think of death with fright.

From their exposure to nineteenth—century literature, Canadians had come to think of death as a relatively comfortable passage to a higher, better life. And so even the prospect of violent death at an early age did not daunt many young Victoria men. "The murderous side of war was distinctly soft-pedalled," writes Robert Nichols, "and . . . insofar as killing cropped up at all, it was allowed to seem a sort of superior deerstalking which, since both sides were at it, must be rather fun."[9] Famous poems such as Tennyson's "Charge of the Light Brigade" had presented suicidal obedience as noble and glorious:

Theirs not to make reply,
Theirs not to reason why,
Theirs but to do and die.

The pages of the *Times* and the *Colonist* are replete with illusions about local "boys'" valor. Both civilian and military poets perpetuated the myth that all Victoria's volunteers were brave and successful. Charles Armstrong wrote, "Victoria's proud of her heroes: "Her soldiers have all made good" (*Colonist*, 1 December 1915, front page, and *Times*, 28 August 1917, 15). When he heard of the death in battle of a close friend, Captain Kenneth George Halley of Salt Spring Island (north of Victoria) wrote, "Smiling at Death . . .

"Fearless you fell . . ." (*Colonist,* 23 September 1915, 5). In 1915, Clive Phillips-Wolley of Victoria (a civilian) wrote that at Ypres in 1915 the Canadians charged "light-hearted into the vortex of Hell."[10] Colonel Lorne Ross of the Western Scots described a young soldier as "facing grim death with courage, "Fearless he fought and fell."[11]

The image of the supernaturally brave Canuck grew out of the romantic rhetoric used by soldier-poets—and their civilian counterparts—and was the product of illusions about what a modern war would be like. Although in some cases soldiers' deaths were accurately described in these poems, the Ross quotation is from the unreliable War Records Office of Max Aitken in London. No doubt the Colonel meant his lines sincerely but they were also useful morale-building material for civilian Canadians, and therefore eminently publishable. Moreover, the image of youths falling painlessly and gallantly was a necessary illusion for civilian readers whose loved ones were in constant peril in the trenches. As well, it is significant that soldiers themselves perpetuated the image of the constantly valiant Canadian serviceman. My readers may believe that much of what was written was naïve or self-deluding. Cynics might even say that these poets were deliberately misled by church, school, military and government propaganda. This is not to malign the genuine courage of Victoria's soldiers, some of whom achieved great feats in the war, but diaries and memoirs as well as the works of military historians such as Desmond Morton suggest that cowardice, desertion and abject terror were not unknown in the Canadian army.

Conquering Berlin

Another one of the illusions which afflicted Victoria people (soldiers and civilians alike) was that the war would be over before Christmas 1914. This widespread naïve optimism led local soldier-poets to be sure that they would soon be marching through Berlin in victory. The conquest of the German Reich was assured for many, including Charles Armstrong, who imagined the "first draft" who left Victoria in August 1914, "fighting, suff'ring, conqu'ring" (*Times*, 28 August 1917, 15)—presumably capturing the German imperial capital itself. While at Valcartier Camp in Québec in September 1914, Robert Harvey of Victoria composed his "Marching Song",

> *Where once we fought the Frenchmen, like brothers now*
> > *we stand*
> *To drive the hated Prussians from out the smiling land;*
> *We'll help them pull his palace about the Kaiser's ears,*
> *The Eighty-Eighth, the Eighty-Eighth Victoria Fusiliers . . . .*

(*Colonist*, 16 September 1914, editorial page)

Leonard McLeod Gould, a former Victoria journalist, wrote that his 102nd Battalion would "rout and beard the Kaiser in his den" (*Colonist*, 16 January 1916, 5). Another soldier-poet, in writing "Goodbye B.C." on his way to the front, declared "Onward we travel determined to win" "Through hosts of the Germans on the way to Berlin" (*Colonist*, 12 June 1915, editorial page). In the same year, an anonymous "Bantam" (in a unit for undersized men), training at Sidney north of Victoria, wrote of his comrades that:

> *They'll get into Berlin some summer eve,*
> *They'll grab old Bill in his golden hall,*
> *After they've smashed his army.*

(*The Bantam Review*, 12 August 1916, 9)

Many of these poets had not yet arrived in France, much less Germany. Looking back, a British volunteer said, "our ignorance was prodigious".[12]

Generations exposed to television images of Americans fighting Viet Cong guerrillas and Canadians in combat with Taliban terrorists may find it inexplicable that Victoria's soldiers were encouraged by civilian poets to see in Flanders knights mounted on prancing chargers. As late as 1916, however, Earl Simonson (a Victoria civilian) could write,

> *The knights come riding, and the purple cup*
> *Is tinged again with silver. Launcelot*
> *Shakes high his fabled blade in the face of Krupp.*

(*Times,* 23 September 1916, 6)

As well, both official recruiting and war loan posters and wartime commercial advertisements presented armored knights on handsome steeds as in medieval epics. As we have seen, Lieutenant-Colonel Beale gave a prominent role to "horsemen" in his "Lay of Liège". In fact, British strategic planners did hope that mounted infantry could achieve a major breakthrough at the front. Canada, moreover, had three regiments of cavalry in the Great War, but they were used rarely. The Fort Garry Horse took part in a charge at the Battle of Cambrai in 1917. "Over the slope came our cavalry", wrote Will Bird in his memoirs, ". . . riding like mad, sabers flashing and lances glittering in perfect formation."[13] From this exploit, only forty men returned.

The Peerless, Piercing Bayonet

Edward Vaughan of the Victoria Fusiliers wrote of "The First C.E.F.", "Hail to the deathless heroes!/The first to draw the blade . . ." (*Times,* 3 August 1917, 7)—before he arrived in France. Victoria's readers might assume that his soldier-comrades were armed with swords and lances and were prepared for warfare as a form of fencing or jousting.

Of course, Canadian soldiers were armed with bayonets. But even here, a romantic haze obscured the reality—even the possibility of—hand-to-hand combat. In 1915, before going overseas, Charles Armstrong eulogized his bayonet:

The Western Scots

> *Without regret*
> *Shall use this perfect piercing pet*
> *Upon the foe who hands are wet*
> *With helpless Belgium's bloody sweat*
> *This pointed perfect, pretty pet—*
> *From old Bayonne—*
> *The Bayonet.*

(*The Western Scot,* 20 November 1915, no. 7, 8)

In another poem, he looked forward to "bayoneting Huns in a ditch" (*Colonist* 31 October 1915, 5). [Fig. III.2] Others were less gruesome and wrote in the popular romantic verbiage. In 1917, one poet, published in the *Times* (15 December, editorial page), referred to the Canadian soldiers' "red'ning steel" which barred "the foe's advance". Both these images were illusory because trench fighters rarely saw the enemy they killed. Throughout the war, the rifle remained the soldier's primary weapon.

Traces of Disillusionment

> *They were young and strong and their hearts were light,*
> *As they cheerily marched away;*
> *Perhaps they recked not a fearful night*
> *Would follow so bright a day.*

With these lines in the *Colonist* on 14 December 1918 (editorial page), an anonymous civilian poet perceived the disillusionment that awaited many Victoria volunteers. As the years passed, some soldiers' published poetry in local newspapers began to exhibit a more realistic, less rhetoric—and illusion-ridden image of their lives in the trenches. Much of their verse was humorous, however, and elided the horrible realities they faced. For example, an anonymous poet told the *Times* on 24 December 1917 (17) about a typical "raid we made on Fritz": while "crawling" and "wriggling" through "No-Man's Land", the soldier

> *. . . could hear the bullets whistle*
> *And the big shells bursting near,*
>
> *Then the sergeant, crawling forward,*
> *Kicked me right behind the ear . . .*
>
> *Now we always have "fixed bayonets"*
> *When we go upon a raid;*
> *Mine got tangled in my trousers*
> *And a nasty gash it made . . .*

Here was a more realistic and truthful image of the trench war. Possibly, the poet believed that the traditional "high diction" or "great rolling phrases"[14] were unsuitable for describing service in a modern war. Of course, he and others were limited by what the public in Victoria (or elsewhere in the country) was allowed to read.

If he ever described his more revolting or frightening experiences in the trenches in a poem or a letter, his statement was censored or not published. Toward 1917 and in 1918, nevertheless, hints of the truth began to appear in published verse—only "hints", however, for censorship concealed the worst.

Victoria's soldier-poets were not alone in their misconceptions. Both the public and the military elite here and in Europe had a misplaced faith in the speed with which railways could get men to the front, the efficacy of machine guns for attack, and the ability of artillery to crush the enemy quickly. Although Canadian military leaders were publicly self-confident in 1914, their assurances to their compatriots were based on lack of experience and of contact with genuine twentieth century armies. The new war would not be short and glorious, and even military strategists ignored the fact that the Crimean War (1853-56), American Civil War (1861-65), and the Boer War (1899-1902) had been longer, bloodier and more bitter than earlier conflicts. If Canada's military and civilian leaders did not understand the new realities, why should the common soldier? I do not deny the sincerity of these writers most of whom, after all, were neither professional soldiers, nor hired hacks, but young (and some older) men who adhered warmly to the ideals of the age and welcomed a war in which they could vicariously or actively express and defend the values which they believed were universally applicable and eternal—and threatened by Germany. If Victoria's recruits in 1914 were deluded about the wonderful adventure that lay ahead of them, they saw their volunteering as, not simply a romantic gesture, but also an unselfish act. If their illusions about the nature of their military service fell away, they continued to believe in defending Canada and its way of life against German tyranny.

2   Fight, Canada, for Empire![1]

In his autobiographical novel, *All Else is Folly,* the Canadian writer Peregrine Acland said of his protagonist, "Not that he was a patriot. Not that he was an Imperialist. He didn't give a damn about the British Empire or any other empire."[2] Judging by both civilian and soldiers' poetry, such sentiments were rare in Victoria. Probably more than other Canadians, volunteers from southern Vancouver Island were filled with imperial patriotism. In short, they were fighting for the integrity of Britain and its Empire, which included Canada. They were not, however, especially imbued with what today we would identify as Canadian national pride. These men felt a commitment to defend relatives in England but also felt a pride and a love for the Empire itself. At its most extreme, some residents of southern Vancouver Island—often former imperial soldiers or bureaucrats—idealized the Empire and even its non-European inhabitants. Ralph Younghusband, born in India, praised native soldiers from the sub-continent who fought in Europe. They knew "how to fight and pray". For him, India was the "mother of warrior sons", "turbaned, subtle, and calm" (*Times,* 13 May, 1918, 19).

Some sceptics might argue that, before and during the conflict, Britain was involved pursuing narrow self-interest and diplomatic intrigue. They might say that British leaders created a false image of Anglo-Saxon virtue affronted by amoral German aggression. Little of this scepticism was evident in Canada and, as far as I can tell, none was found in Victoria.

Moreover, Canadians were confident of British success in any future war. "I had the belief that Britain always won its wars and they were always right," said one Canadian recruit; "This was a feeling that my generation had."[3] Much evidence for this view is found in Victoria's newspapers. An anonymous Canadian poem of 1912 stated of the British people that "As the most progressive people, they are always in the van" (*Colonist,* reprinted in 2 December 1917, 28). The Napoleonic Wars and the Crimean War had all been resolved—or so it seemed—to the credit of the British Empire. The remote South African War had been relatively short and had been touted in the local press as a British victory.

In one way or another, most residents of Victoria considered themselves British. In fact, in the early twentieth century, all Canadians were still legally the subjects of Great Britain. The concept of a distinct Canadian citizenship was a later development and Canada had no independent foreign policy. In fact, at this time, many throughout the white Dominions regarded the whole British Empire as a single state with London as its capital city. Canada's colonial status—at least with regard to foreign and military policy—was clearly enunciated by Prime Minister Wilfrid Laurier in 1910 in the House of Commons: "When Britain is at war," he declared, "Canada is at war." During the 1914-18 conflict, the Canadian government never defined any clear war aims. Prime Minister Robert Borden, however, announced on 1 August 1914 that Canada would "make very sacrifice necessary to ensure the integrity and maintain the honour of our Empire."[4] Most of Victoria's volunteers in 1914, therefore, agreed with Sergeant Leonard McLeod Gould's aim "to serve the King, whom God shall keep from ill" (*Colonist,* 16 January 1916, 5).

In 1914, although most of the officer corps of the first Canadian contingent had been born in Canada, two-thirds of the rank and file who volunteered had been born in Great Britain. 60% of the Second Canadian Division were British born, but the officers again were Canadian.[5] Many of the volunteers were recent

immigrants from the British Isles who welcomed the opportunity
to go home to help their seemingly threatened families, especially
if they could not find work here. Even the native-born identified
strongly with the "old country". In Victoria, the exact number of
British—or locally—born volunteers is hard to determine, because
some local men enlisted elsewhere. However, it is clear that
most of the city's citizens were especially keen to defend Britain
and the Empire. British Columbians as a whole, in fact, showed
the most enthusiasm for the war than any other population of
Canada, offering more than their share of volunteers for the First
Contingent.[6]

Although the anthem "O Canada" dates back to at least 1880
and "The Maple Leaf Forever" to 1867, on 1 September 1914, the
Colonist printed the words to "God Save the King" as "the national
anthem". Its editors followed with Kipling's "The English Flag"
in December 1914; then, "Rule Britannia" in January 1915. An
English poet welcomed Canadians as "lads who, at their Country's
Call, were loyal, brave and true." The soldiers' "country", inferred
the author, was Britain (*Times,* 12 September 1917, 9). This mood
was expressed by the former Federal Minister of Finance, W.S.
Fielding, in a poem published in the *Times* (25 September 1914, 7)
which included the following verse:

> . . . *In the broad world's affairs*
> *Through all the fleeting years,*
> *Since early time*
> *Though 'gainst strong foes arrayed,*
> *Our England undismayed*
> *A gallant part has played*
> *In every clime.*

The dubious historical accuracy of these lines probably did not register withVictoria readers, who were encouraged by the *Times* to sing them to the tune of "God Save the King". As volunteers, therefore, most of Victoria's soldier-poets knew what they were doing—"going to fight for England's glory", as one local poet declared (*Colonist,* 12 August 1914, editorial page). Similarly, another Victoria civilian, Isaac Nixon, wrote in the *Times,* "Ready, Aye, Ready" (12 September 1914, editorial page),

> *The hosts that fought at Waterloo*
> *The sea kings of Trafalgar Bay,*
> *Their blood still throbs in British veins . . .*

Calling up historic memories of the Hundred Years War (1337-1453), Victoria's Robert Harvey, a member the 88th Fusiliers, wrote from Valcartier: "We'll fight as once our fathers did at Crécy and Poitiers" (*Colonist,* 16 September 1914, editorial page). An anonymous civilian poet published in the Times (18 December 1917, editorial page) waxed rapturous over England's military prowess:

> *Glory of thought and glory of deed.*
> *Glory of Hampden and Runnymede;*
> *Glory of ships that sought for goals,*
> *Glory of swords and glory of souls! . . .*
> *Glory transcendent that perishes not—*
> *Hers is the story, hers be the glory—*
> *England!*

These verses were published in Victoria when the war was three years old and showed no sign of ending. Other examples are legion. In a Victory Bond drive, the local poet, Eli Gamlen, appealed to "Victorians! With British hearts and true" (*Times,* 12 November

1917, 10). Dudley Anderson of Victoria extolled the notion of "Imperial Unity" in the *Times* on 7 December 1914, editorial page), stressing that Canada was fighting not for itself alone, but as a loyal colony.

In the minds and verse of soldiers and civilians alike, the "Great" War became a crusade to defend civilization, liberty and Christianity as exemplified by the British Empire. This was a relatively new notion, for the Boer War had not become such an endeavor, although the protection of the "liberty" of South African Britons was often touted as one goal. Now, however, Germany's military and commercial aristocracy seemed to threaten international law and order, whereas the Empire represented a higher form of human culture, which must be defended and even spread around the world.

Nevertheless, in both the *Times* and the *Colonist,* over the years of the war, a decline in references to defending Britain and the British Empire and to the Britishness of Victoria is noticeable. Whereas in 1914, the imperial theme was ubiquitous, after 1915, the drop in frequency was steep, so that the year 1918 saw very few instances of imperial patriotism in verse. In the *Times,* for example, nine poems on "the call of Britain" etc. appeared in September 1914; four in the same month in 1915; two in 1916; one in each of September of 1917 and 1918.

Did Victoria's editors lose interest in Britain or the city's Britishness? Possibly the editors of the *Times,* usually supporters of the Liberals, become alienated from the policies of the ruling Conservatives, which had inaugurated the war effort. Or did they detect a declining interest in their readers? Were local poets simply not submitting verse about British values? Were the wire services not providing suitable material? Or was there, as some historians have claimed, a growing sense that Canada did not need the imperial connection to justify its military pride and national self-sufficiency? Conceivably, anglophone national pride was slowly developing. If so, the pages of the *Times* and the *Colonist* may be evidence for this phenomenon.

3 Some Feeling Against the English

The Newfoundlander Lieutenant Ralph Lewis, although himself loyal to King George and the Empire, noted a 1916 song belted out by newly proud Canadian soldiers: "The Canadians took Courcelette,/ they can fight you just bet . . ."[1] On the other hand, little poetry that was published in Victoria or by local soldiers during the war indicates a great surge in Canadian patriotism. One poem stand out: a hymn to Canada, a place of "hope and freedom", gorgeous scenery and beautiful women (!) by Edward Vaughan (*Times,* 23 October 1916, 13). In the trenches, presumably, Canadians took satisfaction in their undeniable military prowess, and Vaughan proudly refers to how Canadian soldiers at "Ypres' heroic line . . . press[ed] on through shell and mine". But the great national "coming to maturity" which is often said to have occurred after the Battle of Vimy Ridge in April 1917 is not detectable in published verse. (See below).

Perhaps an embryonic Canadian nationalism had already existed among long-established Anglophones such as the descendants of United Empire Loyalists. Such people could be pro-British but could also dislike the British patronizing of "colonials". Moreover, the tide of immigrants from eastern Europe to the prairies had probably loosened imperial loyalties there. Such ties seem to have been slightly diminished in Victoria, but not replaced by hearty Canadian patriotism.

At the front, nevertheless, already in spring of 1915 Field Marshal Douglas Haig detected "Some feeling against the English" among the Canadians.[2] The fighting Canucks wanted to differentiate themselves from the imperial English. They often saw Tommies—and especially their officers—as unbending snobs. Later, especially after the Battle of Vimy Ridge in April 1917, many of Canada's soldiers exhibited a new pride in their professionalism, if not their national identity. "For the first time all four Canadian Corps divisions had attacked as one and their determination and skill carried the day," writes Mark Zuehlke.[3] This proud confidence, however, was not expressed by Victoria's soldier-poets.

To the question, "why did you volunteer?" many a Victoria soldier probably would have answered—possibly unthinkingly, automatically—"to defend the Empire". But a more reflective recruit might have offered several other answers, not always related to either the Empire or the great Dominion in which he lived. Published verse shows that he was motivated by other deeply held and clearly understood "public" values.

4 Bewildered Youths?

Victoria's soldier-poets, as we have seen, were products of their city, province and country a century ago. As such, they expressed the values and attitudes of most local, if less verbally skilled, volunteers—and of their parents, teachers, and leaders. Clearly, whether or not their verses were published in Victoria or elsewhere depended on the whim of the censor. Nevertheless, their poetry reveals what personal qualities were valued by talented young men (graduates of a particular educational system) who were possibly future leaders of their city or country.

"The principles for which you strive are eternal", said Sir Samuel Hughes, Canada's federal Minister of Militia and Defence, in a speech to departing soldiers in October 1914.[1] No doubt Hughes sincerely believed this as did most of his audience who shared with Canadians a confidence in certain "sureties"[2] accepted by the ethical, social and political world of their time, including (as we have seen) the moral grandeur of the British Empire and a sense of the glamor of warfare. The poets' vocabulary sounds strange to Canadians today, not only because it seems overblown but also because it refers to values which we may have come to regard with suspicion or even derision. "Doing one's bit" and "defending the Good" may seem the stuff of older movies, or quaint but deluded values—or worse: ideals corrupted by time, change, and self-serving politicians. But however archaic or misguided such attitudes may seem today, we should not dismiss them as superficial or the poets as hypocritical.

Paul Fussell has suggested that many British soldiers believed that the Great War was a futile exercise and that they were being sent to their deaths for no good cause. This attitude was not totally unknown among Canadian veterans. In 1928, for example, Charles Yale Harrison dedicated his angry, bitter novel *Generals Die in Bed* "to the bewildered youths—British, Australian, Canadian and German—who were killed in that wood a few miles beyond Amiens on August 8th, 1918, . . .".[3]

The published poetry of Victoria's soldiers, however, does not indicate any "bewilderment". As we have seen, many of "our boys" knew what political entity they were defending—at least at the outset of the war—and they had a clear idea of who they were or wanted to be. And so, although we can assume that censorship barred any "negative" poems from being published, the many works of Victoria's soldier-poets were remarkably clear about why their authors went to war. The poems are a compendium of accepted late Victoria and Edwardian public virtues.

The first poems published in Victoria by soldiers are typically filled with enthusiasm over enlistment, the notion of "doing one's bit" for a good cause and going off on a "great adventure". Their response to training (often at the Willows Camp, later at Valcartier), however, is negatively critical, and gradually some disillusionment with the mundane details of military service is heard. In their verses, references to the glory of soldiering declined, but most soldier-poets remained committed to the purpose of the war. If they were homesick for Victoria or horror-struck by the violence of the trenches, these feelings rarely appeared in poetry accepted and published. Nevertheless, soldiers' verse presented much else that might be disconcerting to readers on the home front, as we shall see.

Most often, what Victoria's civilians read of soldiers' verse was humorous and light-hearted. "Keep Smiling" was a popular theme and the importance of regular food, cigarettes and fresh clothing was stressed. In the trenches, dogged optimism and creature comforts were of the utmost importance. And so the verse we encounter in Victoria's newspapers and journals and in their regimental newsletters was probably more truly representative of the mood of the trench soldiers than the angry despair of the English poets Owen or Sassoon.

Fighting the Forces of Evil

Our great-grandfathers believed that they were fighting the German army as the embodiment of Evil. Throughout the media of the Western allies, the Great War became a morality tale in which virtuous knights triumphed over forces of the Devil. In Victoria, John Murray (a civilian poet) defined the Germans, Austrians, Bulgarians and Turks, as "the Devil's quarter of nations, performing his work" (*Colonist,* 12 January 1917, editorial page). The German invasion of Belgium and the atrocities attributed to the Germans motivated many local "knights". After the Second Battle of Arras in 1917, Sergeant Gould wrote that ". . . From their tottering stronghold/The Forces of Evil are hurled."[4] Elsewhere, he wrote that the men of his 102nd Battalion were "willing to lay down their lives,/ To battle for the weak, to right the wrong" (*Colonist,* 16 January 1916, 5). Paradoxically, this moralistic attitude could co-exist with a respectful, almost comradely, opinion of the ordinary German soldier. (See below.)

Defending Freedom

In Paul Fussell's view, the notion of defending the invaded Belgians and French and therefore defending liberal democracy did not motivate most soldiers. But among the more literate and alert Canadian soldiers—at least in the first months of the war—the concept of political freedom was tied up with imperial patriotism and Christianity, a muddled potpourri of beliefs, but doubtlessly sincere. From Atlantic Canada, for example, Lieutenant Ralph Lewis wanted to "go and strike another blow for King and Empire, Liberty and God."[5] Similarly at the western end of Canada, defending Britain was equated with supporting "Freedom". Even if not well-read, Victoria's soldiers had learned to regard slogans such as "defending liberty" and "preserving freedom" as mantras. Rudyard Kipling was the first major poet to identify Britain's war aim as a defence of "liberty" in a poem in the London *Times* reproduced in the Victoria *Colonist* on 3 September 1914, 2).

Similarly, Victoria's Dudley Anderson envisioned the colonies and Dominions all united "in the cause of liberty" (*Times,* 7 December 1914, editorial page). These concepts did not mean democracy as we know it today; i.e. universal suffrage for both men and women or social equality. For the poets and their readers, "liberty" entailed the right of subjects of the British Empire not to be governed by a foreign power, especially Germany. Independence or even self-government, of course, did not apply to the non-white peoples of the Empire. And yet, paradoxically, those who revered "liberty" also assumed that Britain had a mission "to make men free" (*Times,* 18 December 1917, editorial page), which prefigures the later proselytizing crusades of several American governments.

And so, during the 1917 conscription crisis, the civilian John Murray of Victoria wrote:

> *Think of this, freemen, think it over again—*
> *Would you live under the Kaiser as serfs? . . .*
> *Could you live and groan 'neath the heel of the Hun?*
> *If you could let him win the war;*
> *Then your freedom along with your place in the sun*
> *Would vanish like a shooting star.*

(*Times,* 12 September 1917, 3)

Soldier-poets had already taken up this theme. Edward Vaughan of Victoria extolled the Canadian Expeditionary Force in the "The First C.E.F.":

> *The crimson banners swelling*
> *On every wind that blows*
> *Hold firm the cause of Freedom*
> *Against unnumbered foes . . . .*

Hail to the deathless heroes!
The first to draw the blade;
Their lives and homes and loved ones
On Freedom's altars laid.

(*Times,* 4 August 1917, 7)

In the same mood, Colonel Lorne Ross of the Western Scots imagined a dead soldier having "heard the voice of Empire", and "for Freedom . . . shed his blood."[6]

Will-Less Robots?

The novelist Harrison wrote that, in his experience, "Months of training . . . have stiffened us. We must carry on, carry on . . . In a thousand ways this has been drilled into our heads. A thousand trivial rules . . . have made will-less robots of us all."[7] On the other hand, the soldiers James Pedley and Will Smith describe small acts of insubordination by independent-minded young Canadians, actions which were occasionally tolerated by their officers. Doubtless every soldier knows that, upon enlisting, he or she forfeits many private concerns and aspirations. This sacrifice is part of the personal integrity which they wish to maintain in their profession or, in our poets' cases, their temporary calling. The real attitude of Victoria's soldier probably lies somewhere between Harrison's despair and Pedley and Smith's subdued anarchy.

The poets recognized limits to the individual's personal freedom. The need to do what one conceived as one's duty was widespread in the culture of our great-grandparents. In Victoria, at least, appeals to the "Patriotic Fund" and to buy war bonds reminded civilians that they had a "duty to perform". Certainly the poems submitted by Victoria's soldiers are full of references to "doing one's bit". Typically, Charles Armstrong noted that many a local volunteer had "given up home, wife and kiddies" He's manfully doing his bit" (*Colonist*, 1 December 1915, front page, in a frame). Donald Goodspeed noted that Canadian schools had "produced implicit obedience", with the result that it would be surprising if large scale resistance to enlisting had occurred. Moreover, he wrote, "Canadians had never been to war before [sic] and for all they knew this was the way things had to be."[8] Moreover, the new workplaces in an industrializing society required trained and disciplined laborers, so that, for many of Victoria's working class soldiers, the trenches must have seemed like just another job demanding already inculcated virtues. Of course, it is worth noting that many a volunteer joined because it was the lesser of two evils. Not to volunteer could result in shaming so that some men faced "no choice at all".[9] This situation is rarely described in soldiers' verse.

Modris Eksteins maintains, however, that by 1917 the word "duty" had disappeared from the poetry of British trench soldiers.[10] Victoria's soldier-poets, on the other hand, did not abandon the concept, although they did not use the word as often in the years 1917-18 as they had done earlier. Their humor becomes blacker and their stoicism fatalistic but, when they write of "carrying on" and "playing the game", they may be simply using a less bombast-laden word than "duty". It is also possible that editors had begun to be wary of such vocabulary. Nevertheless, as we have seen, in 1917 Aitken's *Canada in Khaki* published Colonel Ross' memorial to a Canadian soldier who "followed Duty's guidance".[11] The Canadian War Records Office, of course, had a vested interest in perpetuating morale-building exercises.

Supporting Conscription

Given their pride in "doing their duty", Victoria's soldier-poets favored conscription, a fact which is corroborated by evidence from the front. They voted for the Union government of Robert Borden in the election of late 1917, knowing that, if victorious, he would introduce compulsory military service. Most Canadian servicemen would have agreed with the verses printed in the *Times* (29 November 1917, 7) entitled "Somewhere in France":

> *Often in my trench I think*
> *Of the poor chaps left at home,*
> *Of the perils that surround them*
> *Wherever they may roam . . .*
>
> *How awful it must be at night*
> *To be in a feather bed*
> *Or find for breakfast when you rise*
> *There's butter on your bread . . . .*

(Britain introduced conscription in 1916.)

A regular theme of Victoria soldier-poets' verse was the castigation of "slackers". For example, Edward John Rashleigh of the BC Bantams, training at Sidney, asked

> *Are you the guy that's seen at the dance,*
> *Dressed in "civvies"—won't take the chance*
> *To prove you're a man, as the others have done,*
> *And get into khaki and shoulder a gun?*
> *Are you?*

(*Bantam Review,* 12 August 1916, 8)

Letters and diaries suggest that this view was widespread. Doubtless, most Victoria soldiers welcomed Ottawa's introduction of compulsory military service in 1917.

Following "Guts-and-Gaiters"

The generals of the Great War have come in for damning indictments, notably Lloyd George's contemporary epithet, "donkeys". Today's assessment is more balanced. Many historians maintain, however, that, confronted with unprecedented problems, most military leaders initially failed the test. The exception is Canada's Sir Arthur Currie, a former Victoria real estate dealer and militia gunner who had commanded the 50th Highlanders. Having succeeded Field Marshal Julian Byng as head of the Canadian Corps in 1915, he had learned from the French the importance of careful reconnaissance and the briefing of even the lowest ranking trench soldier. As well, he insisted on measures which would reduce casualties among his men.

His pear-shaped physique, however, was a liability. Weighing 250 pounds and standing at six foot four inches, with a stentorian voice, some of his men nicknamed him "Guts-and-Gaiters"[12] Worse, he was given to pompous utterances which recycled all the rhetorical bombast of the early war poetry. For example, on 17 March 1918, he issued an "Order to the Canadian Army Corps", in which he addressed his troops:

> *You will not die but step into immortality. Your mothers will not lament your fate but will be proud to have born such sons. Your names will be revered forever and ever by your grateful country and God will take you unto Himself.*[13]

Already skeptical of traditional religious "up-lift", his listeners regarded this message with cynicism. In fact, Morton and Granatstein aver that he "was not loved by his men."[14]

Nevertheless, some of Victoria's soldier-poets—at least those whose work was published—did not seem to care how he looked in uniform or how he sounded on a parade ground. When Currie visited Victoria in the fall of 1919, accolades to this former resident of the capital poured forth. One anonymous poet (possibly a veteran) hailed Currie as a "true knight" with a "strict regard for justice", led on his "silent way" by "stern Duty" (*Colonist*, 10 September 1919, editorial page). A returned soldier, James H. Brewton of Victoria, dedicated a long poem "To General Sir Arthur W. Currie", which begins,

> *We hail thee! Leader of those—our sons*
> *Who pledged their lives upon the fields of France:*
> *And, daring all, went forward those long years,*
> *Leaving a name a glory that will live*
> *Imperishable. Not glory did they seek,*
> *Their goal the World's redemption,*
> *And a Peace that would be always . . .*

(*Colonist*, 5 October 1919, editorial page)

The poem ignores rhyme and meter and is in a free verse form, suggesting the changes coming in poetry in the early twentieth century but it still revels in high diction of the pre- and war years—"bugles", "laurels", "glory" etc.—denoting that this form of expression still had meaning for many Victoria people. On his brief return to the city in 1919, Currie was presented with a silver tray by Premier John Oliver and a banquet in his honor was held at the legislative buildings.

These poems, while bombastic and suitable for public morale-raising, contain an accurate assessment of Currie's abilities. Perhaps, upon reflection, Victoria's soldier-poets recognized that "Guts-and-Gaiters" had helped them to win the war and saved their lives, too.

Judging from the published verse, even if a Victoria soldier did not care much about the British Empire or Canadian pride, even if concepts such as "the good", "duty" and "freedom" were not in his personal lexicon, maintaining his self-respect helped him to "carry on". Far from being "bewildered", he had a sense of personal honor which involved being courageous and "masculine". In particular, he wanted to be "a good sport".

5 A Soldier's Private Values

The poetry of Victoria's soldiers is replete with references to their personal values. Some readers will say that these statements were about ideals to be lived up to rather than descriptions of actual practice, and they may be correct. Moreover, it is likely that not every single Victoria soldier adhered to all these values. Nevertheless, training in the classroom, in church and in the army itself excluded alternate views or opinions in the minds of most recruits, even if they joined up mainly for adventure or an income.

And so, as this study suggests, their verse is a document of the personal standards of many men and also asks of our twenty-first century culture: "do we still hold to these ideals?"

Honorable Men

Writing during the Great War, BC poet Loftus McInnes wrote,

> *How often have we heard the cynics prate*
> *Of our proud empire toppling in decay,*
> *Our youth grown sickly and degenerate*
> *And valour with our grandsires passed away . . . .*[1]

The "cynics" need not have worried. Our soldier-poets were much concerned with the concept of "honor", a vague term perhaps, but one which implied—at the very least—a man's reputation for morally upright behavior. Not surprisingly they associated it with the good name of Great Britain as well. For example, Fusilier Edward Vaughan wrote of Canadian volunteers:

> *They rose at honor's bidding*
> > *To save the land from shame.*
> *Their names shall live forever*
> > *On Britain's roll of fame.*

(*Times,* 4 August 1917, 7)

Honor, however, also involved physical courage, other "masculine" qualities and a sense of fair play.

When Hell's on the Earth . . .

. . . an honorable man was brave. At least two Victoria soldier-poets expressed particular admiration for the runners who carried messages from trench to trench. Sergeant Gould wrote "The Runners. An Appreciation. (Inspired by the Runners of the 102nd Canadian Infantry Battalion)", part of which reads:

When wires are broken, and pigeons won't fly,
When shrapnel and whiz-bang are bursting on high,
When hell's on the earth, and earth's in the sky;
Who are the boys who will get through or die?
    The Runners.

(*Canada in Khaki,* Vol. I, 20)

In "Somewhere in France", Sergeant Sheldon-Williams praised "The Runners of the Somme" who, faced with danger, would simply "light up another weird issue fag" and "carry on."[2] On the other hand, in reality few soldiers were the fearless heroes described in published verse. Local civilian poets might declare than Victoria "boys" died "smiling at death" (see above), but "there are times," wrote Lieutenant Lewis of Nova Scotia's 25th Battalion, "when the bravest of us get the creeps."[3] The historian Desmond Morton is more explicit: "Even outstanding soldiers felt crippled by terror."[4] As we have already seen, written expression of such fear was impossible both to the soldier concerned to support his own and his family's image of him, and to his editors at home, who were mandated to buttress public morale. Moreover, any overt expression of fear would have been a shameful contrast to the volunteers' 1914 image of themselves valiantly going off to fight nobly for justice and "the Good", and was considered unmanly.

God's Test of Manhood

In his memoir, Lieutenant James Pedley of Toronto wrote that, upon reaching France, "I felt proud that I was at last [. . . at . . .] the front; at last filled a man's part in the war play."[5] Conceivably, his relief had been conditioned by civilian verse and song which loudly stressed the manliness of the volunteer. In November 1914, at the Royal Theatre in Victoria, one could attend "Marching Orders or Shoulder to Shoulder. A Grand Military Musical Review" and hear the song, "To Make a Man out of You". The lyrics describe a young lady who "walks out" only with men who have volunteered.[6] An anonymous poem in Victoria's *The Week* (16 December 1916, 2) was entitled "A Mother's View . . . Will He Come Back?" and included the view, "God's test of manhood is I know/Not 'Will he come [back]?' but 'did he go?'" Similarly, Frank Burrell, a Victoria civilian, urged local youths to "Quit you like men!" (*Colonist*, 9 February 1915, editorial page). [Fig.II.5.1]

With these civilian voices in their ears, the soldier-poets, like most enlisted men, assumed that all able-bodied males would join up. Edward John Rashleigh, in training at the Sidney camp, urged the man in "civvies/ . . . To prove you're a man, as the others have done,/And get into khaki and shoulder a gun" (Bantam Review, 12 August 1916, 8). "Won't you join and be a man?" asked Sergeant Gould of men who would not volunteer (*Colonist*, 5 February 1916, 5). The "white feather" campaign was calculated to stress the un-manly qualities of men who apparently had not volunteered. (Women would pin white feathers on males in civilian clothes.) The authorities deplored such actions and they were castigated even by Sergeant Sheldon-Williams in a generous poem, "The False Focus", wherein he derided "silly girl-children [who] giggle and gloat", having unjustly shamed a man who could not volunteer (*Colonist*, 8 September, 1915, 12). Nevertheless, the "girl-children" expressed a widely-held opinion.

Fig.II.5.1: "Here's Your Chance. It's Men we Want"

A recruiting poster, appealing to men who wanted to prove or to test their "masculinity", one of many motives Victoria's males had for joining up. (Archives of Ontario War Poster Collection. C 233-2-0-4-200.)

Many men were concerned to prove their masculinity by not complaining about discomfort or even wounds. And so their poetry tended to downplay any physical misery, fear or loneliness they may have felt. But more was involved than mere stoicism. They had to be both good at sports and "good sports".

Good Sports and Good Sportsmen

As the nineteenth century waned, the increasingly urban world—even in Victoria—was regarded as "soft, vice-ridden, and alienating."[7] (Loftus McInnes, quoted above, had heard this criticism). Accordingly, violent contact sports such as soccer had been encouraged because they were believed to develop what were presumably traditional manly qualities. Typically, said the soldier-poet Gould, the men who joined the 102nd Battalion were "trained to war by aptitude in games" (*Colonist,* 16 January 1916, 5). In 1914, the view was widespread that sport and military service were closely related experiences. Throughout the British Empire, educators believed that sport would give "a young man the body of a Greek and the soul of a Christian knight."[8] Many, in fact, assumed that, at the very least, proficiency in sport would equip a youth with a sense of "fair play". Late in the war, draftees arriving at the Willows Camp were described three times in one article by a *Times* journalist as being "good sports" (January 4, 1918, editorial page). The term occurs many times in the local poetry and prose of the Great War.

Consequently, our great-grandparents regarded the military life as akin to engaging in outdoor games. The poem "Vitai Lampada" (The Torch of Life) by Sir Henry Newbolt was well known throughout the Empire. On a 1923 tour of Canada where it was still popular. the poet was constantly asked to recite it. In the first stanza, he imagined a cricket coach urging his men to "Play up! Play up! And play the game!" The second verse presented an officer encouraging his soldiers in a desert battle. The third suggested that any former schoolboy, once grown up, would know that "playing the game" meant carrying out one's duty honorably, faithfully and unselfishly.[9] Typically, this attitude held that the Boers' guerrilla tactics in the South African War were "unsporting". Even after the middle of the twentieth century, the motto of my high school in Victoria was "play the game".

Civilian writers here often used the metaphor of "playing the game" to describe military service. In September 1914, finding that "our flag is threatened east and west", R.E. Clark wrote that "We've buckled on our swords" and "We'll play them at their game" (*Colonist*, 2 September 1914, editorial page). Consequently, many volunteers saw the 1914 war as just another outdoor game—but on a larger scale. The enemy was seen as an opponent, not as a deadly adversary. Participation in battle would be like a good cricket or baseball game, hard work but fun.

And so the outbreak of war in the summer of 1914 challenged the sporting instincts of young males in Victoria, a view encouraged by local newspaper editors and poets. An anonymous poem on the *Times'* editorial page for 14 September 1914 urged volunteers to "help Old Britain", if necessary to "like a British soldier die", and to "nobly 'play the game'." Another poem, "The Attack" by a British soldier, appeared on the *Times'* editorial page, 6 July 1915. After an assault on the German trenches,

> *The men get to work with bayonet,*
> *And win the hard-played game.*

The use of the sporting and "fair play" metaphor continued throughout the war. Some women shared this attitude. Victoria's Blanche Holt Murison counselled Canadians

> ... *to serve,*
> *Unmindful of the tide of praise or blame:* ...
> *To stand the test—to play and win the game.*[10]

Soldiers were often commended for their sportsmanlike qualities, which meant honoring the accepted rules of a game. In a poem in memoriam, a veteran, J.L.Vallie, commended his old friend Flight Lieutenant Joe Gorman as "A sportsman always, worthy of the name,/A clean, consistent player of the game" (*Times*, 21 December 1917, editorial page).

Even after the war, the well-known English poet Siegfried Sassoon declared—more realistically than the above poets—that "war's a bloody game", in his poem "Aftermath", published in the *Colonist* (10 September 1919, editorial page). Locally, the grieving family of Raymond S. MacDonald of the Gordon Highlanders, killed in action on October 22, 1918, offered the *Colonist* three lines:

> *In the silent halls of fame*
> *One line we gave for him,*
> *"He played the game".*

(22 October 1919, 6)

Our Work's Not Done

As the war dragged on in a never-ending stalemate, however, Victoria's soldier-poets made less mention of the values of honor, courage, and "manliness". Nevertheless, they claimed still to believe in the necessary defeat of Germany. Only if that happened could their sufferings be justified. "Long before 1918," writes Morton, "most Canadian soldiers had lost any enthusiasm for the war, but they had not changed their minds that it must be won."[11] Even Halley's poem inspired by the Battle of Courcelette, quoted above, which presents a vivid account of trench warfare, ends with these three lines:

> But I'd rather fall at my country's call than be one who
>   stayed away.
> Our work's not done, it has just begun, in spite of the
>   thousands gone,
> So we leave you here, and your duty's clear—it's for you
>   to "carry on".

(*Colonist*, 16 December 1916, editorial page)

If such confidence was being tested, on the other hand, it is rarely evident in soldiers' poetry published in Victoria. Of course, one may ask if these last lines were a coda "tacked on" to the end of the poem, inserted to please the censors and to appease the folks back home. This is hard to know without interviewing the poets themselves, now an impossible task. Despite the demoralizing effects of battle, the poet Halley claimed to believe that a purpose still existed, stressing the traditional call of "duty", and, despite the realism of the description, it's clear that he—as many other Canadian soldiers—still believed in the Allied cause, if only because to do so made their ordeals purposeful.

6   Grub, Tobacco . . . and Rum

Maintaining their personal integrity was a struggle for Canadian soldiers, especially if they were disillusioned with the British connection, or less inclined to support certain values such as "doing one's duty". As far as the published poetry reveals, however, many of Victoria's soldiers seem to have succeeded in retaining some self—respect. Still, masculine pride and the necessity to "carry on" are hard to sustain with permanently wet feet or a daily dose of new lice. Fortunately, Victoria's poets in uniform were helped by a regular supply of certain "creature comforts". At the Willows and other local training camps and especially in the trenches they looked forward to parts of their meals and treasured their alcohol and their tobacco.

Rations

"After breakfast we got our issue of rum, which was rather small," said one Canadian, "but we don't need rum to fight, all we need is grub and cigarettes."[1] Some of Victoria's soldiers would have disagreed about the rum, but most would have supported the idea that good and regular food (including sweets) and a steady supply of tobacco made "living in a sewer"[2] somewhat bearable. Dinner in the trenches might consist of tea, a tin of pork and beans, corned beef or stew, biscuits and butter or fruit jam. Mutton and beef were rare. "Rations . . . are up and down," wrote Private Donald Fraser; "at the best they are never too plentiful. The tendency is to be on the scrimp side."[3] Victoria's soldier-poets confirm these impressions. Consequently, they relied heavily on packages from home, especially if they contained jam. Private Edward Vaughan, with Victoria's 88th Battalion, described one aspect of the situation well:

> We've plenty of bully beef, biscuits and tea,
> We get enough cheese for to block up the sea;

We shave in the marmalade tins by the score;
The sight of a bean tin no more we can bear.
We've bacon for breakfast and butter for tea,
To build of the bully a dugout we plan—
Yet still there's a question arises to me—
But what has become of the Strawberry Jam?

(*Colonist*, 19 July 1917, editorial page) Often what was officially labeled "strawberry jam" was watery, made with figs and artificially flavored. At the same time, soldiers were suspicious if strawberry jam turned up when unexpected because this meant that they would be going "over the top" that night. [Fig.II.6.1]

Fig.II.6.1: "Coward's Supreme Chocolate"

This advertisement may seem to trivialize the trench experience, but does not exaggerate the soldier's concern for regular meals, including treats. (*Victoria Daily Times*, 5 June 1918, 11.)

During and after the heat of battle, the soldier because thirsty, but the water provided often seemed undrinkable because it was clumsily chlorinated by the "M.O.s" (Medical Officers). This necessary health measure gave the water a distinctive, unpleasant taste. Lieutenant Charles Armstrong lamented, in part:

At meals I have my tea with thee,
  Chlorine!
With soup, with fish with ev'ry dish—
  Chlorine!
Yet, while I'm faithful thus to thee,
  Chlorine!
Another claims thy constancy
  Chlorine!
You love, I know, our fell M.O.
  Chlorine! . . .
Ah, wanton! When this war if o'er,
  Chlorine!
I pray I'll never see thee more,
  Chlorine!

(*Canada in Khaki,*** vol. I, 168)**

Nickyteen

Robert Service imagined a "Tommy" declaring, "I'd like to say, in a general way,/There's nothing like Nickyteen . . ."[4] The Canadian military historian Tim Cook refers to the "raging nicotine addiction" which prevailed the trenches.[5] Private Harry Clarke, a Victoria soldier, working with the No. 1 Field Ambulance of the British Expeditionary Force, explained how, when a wounded man was brought in, "he gets a shot of anti-tetanus serum to prevent lockjaw; then cocoa, and lastly a cigarette" (*Colonist,* 14 July 1916, 5).

Fig.II.6.2: "The choicest gifts go up in smoke".

Tobacco, like rum, was almost a necessity for the trench soldier. The image says it all. (*Canada in Khaki,* (London: Cassell and Company, 1917). Vol. II), 150.

Even more essential to the soldiers' well-being than sweet condiments, therefore, was "nickyteen". [Fig.II.6.2] Volunteers gave out cigarettes to soldiers as they left home by train. At the front, tobacco was part of the weekly rations. Of course, the dangers inherent in tobacco-smoking paled in comparison with what the soldier faced in the trench or just "over the top". Moreover, the sharing of cigarettes was part of the fellowship of misery. In the *Colonist,* a soldier-poet, the semi-anonymous "J.A.A.", wrote in part,

> *. . . If it is fate that in battle we fall,*
> *And death hovers o'er us, we hear the last call,*
> *We shan't fear the shadows, our hard luck forget,*
> *If between our set teeth we've a last cigarette.*

(*Colonist,* 11 July 1915, editorial page)

Of course, when newspapers featured such "up-beat" verse on their editorial pages, they confirmed local readers' belief that "the boys" were bearing up well under the stress of battle.

Tobacco was the proverbial two-edged sword. Although inhaling the smoke of strong cigarettes could mask unpleasant trench odors, at night red cigarette embers drew sniper fire. Consequently, soldiers were often ordered to extinguish all cigarettes after dark. Nearly every soldier was a chain-smoker, which relieved stress and boredom, but which also caused "trench cough", exacerbated by the constant damp.

Soldiers' Real Delight [6]

"Some fellows spend a terrible amount on booze," wrote the young Harold Innis (later a well-known Canadian political economist) in his diary in 1916.[7] [Fig.II.6.3] Drunkenness plagued the Canadian Expeditionary Force and led to more courts martial than all other misdemeanors combined. In training on Salisbury Plain in England, much carousing occurred, with the resulting infractions of rules. Alcohol abuse among soldiers was a problem in Victoria as well as overseas. Soldiers training at "the Willows" made popular the nearby Willows Hotel, the only liquor outlet in the area until Prohibition closed it in 1917. One private in the Western Scots, training at the Willows camp, described the situation explicitly:

> *The Frenchman loves his native wine,*
> *The German drinks his beer,*
> *The Englishman takes his half-and-half*
> *Because it brings good cheer;*
> *The Yankee drinks his whiskey straight,*
> *Because it gives him dizziness,*

Fig.II.6.3:

There is a jar we love to see,	The prim old maids may agitate,
Which bears the letters S.R.D.;	And 'gainst rum sing a hymn of hate;
Of all the rations in the cart,	Let them rave on—for what care we?
It's dearest to the soldier's heart . . .	We watch and wait for S.R.D.
(*Canada in Khaki*, Vol. II, 70.)	

(*The Forty-Niner,* 1.4, 23. (49th Battalion [Edmonton Regiment]); also Tim Cook, *At The Sharp End. Canadians Fighting the Great War 1914-1918* (Toronto: Viking, 2007), 243.

> *But the Canadian has no choice at all*
> *And drinks the whole d—business!*

(*The Western Scot,* 26 January 1916, 2)

James Robertson (also of the Western Scots) was probably the poet who acknowledged the alcohol-induced discipline problems of soldiers stationed at the Willows Camp:

> *It's true that we sometimes kick over the trace,*
> *(Resulting in fourteen days "C.B." to face—*
> *Gives one time to get dry*
> *For more by and by),*
> *P'r'aps it's only a failing for "fun"*
> *Or a touch of ennui,*
> *Sets us off on the spree,*
> *We'll be there when there's work to be done.*

(*The Western Scot,* 4 December 1915, 6)

"C.B." refers to the punishment "Confined to Barracks". Robertson may have also been the "J.R." who voiced the pride of the "Sick Berth" men—who reveled in a name used in the British navy—

> *We're only "Poultice Wallopers" a-bringing up the rear;*
> *But in prompt "first aid" or at "sick parade", when your*
> *works are out of gear.*
> *You bless the "No. 9" that cured effects of last night's*
> *beer . . .*

(*Western Scot,* 4 December 1915, 6)

Wherever soldiers trained, relief was found in a nearby pub. In his memoir of the 102nd Battalion, Leonard McLeod Gould included

"The Song of the Spit" ("Sung to the tune of 'John Brown's Body'.") One verse indicated why alcohol was so necessary at the Comox Spit Camp, north of Victoria on Vancouver Island:

> *The sand gets in our blankets, and the wind blows chill*
> *   and drear.*
> *If life was dull at Comox, it's a damned sight duller here,*
> *You have to go a mile or so to get a glass of beer,*
> *   As we go marching on.*[8]

At his training camp on Salisbury Plain in England, a Victoria soldier parodied Thomas Gray's "Elegy in a Country Churchyard" with references to the boozy antics of his comrades. Earlier I have quoted his opus which concludes, "The paths of pleasure lead but to the clink" (*Colonist*, 23 June 1917, editorial page).

On the other hand, in the trenches, a regular allotment of rum may have been a virtual necessity. For many, including Victoria's servicemen, it provided a sense of well-being, however temporary. Tim Cook writes that "liquid courage protected men from physically and psychologically crumbling under the rigours of trench warfare".[9] Rum helped to combat the cold and physical exhaustion and aided in sleep after combat. Sometimes it was added to the tea in the morning and, before an attack, a double tot of rum was served. Needless to say, most soldiers scorned the prohibitionists. Private John Mynott, also at the Willows Camp, proposed a toast:

> *Here's to a temperance supper*
> *   With water in glasses tall,*
> *And coffee and tea to end with—*
> *   And me not there at all.*

(*The Western Scot*, 26 January 1916, 2)

The editor of Victoria's *The Week* received a poem written "by a man in the trenches 'Somewhere in France', when he heard that Alberta had voted 'dry'" (23 October 1915, editorial page):

> . . . *Preachers over in Canada*
> *Who rave about Kingdom Come*
> *Ai'nt pleased with our ability*
> *And are wanting to stop our rum.*
>
> *Water, they say, would be better*
> *Water: Great Scott! Out here*
> *We're up to our knees in water*
> *Do they think we are standing in beer?*

The weekly's editor thought so much of these sentiments that he reprinted them on 26 August 1916. The poet's point of view struck a chord with servicemen in Victoria, for these verses also appeared in *The Timber Wolf* (27 May 1916, n.p), the journal of the 103rd Battalion based then at the Victoria armories. In general, most soldiers did not support prohibition, although it later became law. (After a referendum, British Columbia introduced prohibition on 1 October 1917. It was repealed on 15 June 1921.)

Most Victoria soldiers would probably have agreed with one Canuck who said jokingly, "if we hadn't had our rum, we would have lost the war."[10] Such humor was as vital as food, tobacco and alcohol to the serviceman's emotional survival.

7 Many a Laugh

Traditionally, men in military service have resorted to humor to relieve the irritations and boredom of barracks life and the terrors of battle. In 1919 a student of recent soldiers' verse found their poetry "less grim than that of the civilian singers. Much of it is even jovial."[1] The famous British war poets, the novelists, and historians such as Paul Fussell have given us the impression that most British soldiers were a solemn lot. What about Victoria's soldiers? In postwar times, our veterans seemed to prefer to recall service incidents that were amusing—probably a universal phenomenon. Judging by what was published, however, Victoria's soldiers wrote fewer bloodthirsty and hate-filled poems than did their relatives, friends and fellow citizens at home in the suburbs of Oak Bay or Esquimalt.

From some of the foregoing excerpts, it's clear that many soldiers had a sense of humor and expressed it in their verse. Especially cheerful in tone were the regimental newsletters, wherein, with some exceptions, are found only "up-lifting" and often very funny poems. Of course, editors of Victoria's civilian newspapers and journals were mandated to publish such poems which suggested that Victoria's "boys" were all bravely enduring life in the trenches.

Certainly, faced with their first experience of military training (for which most were completely unprepared), recruits needed a sense of the ridiculous. One soldier "at a western school"—probably Victoria's Willows Camp—wrote about the stupidities he found every day. "Making a Soldier" ran to six exasperated verses on the editorial page the *Times,* on 4 September 1914. Part of the poem described a subaltern's response to drill:

> *So he held his head, as they say in the book*
> *As if he was having his picture took.*
> *Then he closed his heels and clamped his knees*
> *And slapped his hands, at the stand at ease,*
> *He twisted his neck in a soldier's kink*
> *He fixed his eyes, and ceased to wink.*
> *But his weary brain did nothing but think*
> *What the h—is the use of all this?*

The second verse ended,

> *The sergeant instructor, so bronzed and grey,*
> *With his pacing stick followed him night and day,*
> *But beneath his breath God heard him say:*
> *"What a d . . . . . old fool the man is . . ."*

Something of the inadequacy of Canadian training and of the volunteers' reputation for indiscipline may be apparent in this poem. In late 1914 such criticisms could be published because Ottawa's official censor had not yet been appointed. [Fig.II.7.1] As well, the *Times* was less strait-laced than the *Colonist.*

Fig.II.7.1: "Eyes Left"

"And when I say 'Eyes left', I want to see those eyes come over with a click." The cartoonist, Herbert Ernst McRitchie (1896-1919) had been a law student at the University of Saskatchewan. He served with the Canadian Army Medical Corps. (*Canada in Khaki.* Vol. I, 22.)

Desmond Morton and Glenn Wright have written that "a winter of wet canvas, route marches and pre-dawn physical training in Victoria" could produce pneumonia or rheumatism.[2] This is evident in at least one locally written poem. In December 1918, Rifleman D.B. Shepherd of the 258th Battalion, Canadian Rifles, was encamped at "the Willows", recruited to be part of the Allied intervention force in revolutionary Russia. Undeterred by the prospect of war in Siberia, he wrote to the *Times* about a more pressing peril. One verse reads:

> *We like your charming city*
>   *On this soft Pacific slope,*
> *When our Eastern snap is over,*
>   *We'll come again, we hope.*
> *We love your snow-capped mountains,*
>   *Each city, street and lane,*
> *But tell me, some old resident,*
>   *Does it always, always, rain?*

(*Times*** 14 December 1918, 7) (Fig.II.7.2]**

Another rifleman, D. Macksen of the 260th Battalion Canadian Rifles, took Shepherd to task for whining, reminding him that "the boys in France have fought for years . . . /And didn't stop because of rain . . ." (*Times,* 19 December 1918, 6).

Fig.II.7.2: The Willows Camp, Victoria, c. 1914-1918.

Winter rains made tent accommodation uncomfortable. Even on this sunny day, puddles and mud are evident in the lower left foreground. (Private Collection)

In 1916 one writer presented a poem entitled "The Survivor" in which he claims to have met a "Private bold" at the Willows Camp. This man claimed to be "the Major and Subalterns four/ The Captain . . . "And the Cook of the Company Mess". He went on to assert that he was "the Piquets, the Guards and Fatigues," The prisoners in their cell, "The Sergeant gruff and the Corporal bluff . . ."; the visitor

> *. . . pondered, you see, how this wonder could be,*
> *And this man with these ranks who'd endow*
> *Till he said with great glee, "I'm the only one free*
> *From the mumps in my Company now."*

(Colonist, 20 February 1916, 10) Typically, the jaunty tone of such poems contributed to the notion that Victoria's volunteers were generally a happy bunch, which was possibly true in the early years of the war. One may be sceptical, however, when a later article in the *Times* on January 4, 1918 (editorial page), insisted that "many a laugh, but never a grumble" was heard among the conscripts in No. 2 Depot at the Willows Camp. Using the approved jargon, this journalist maintained the draftees were all "good sports to a man".

In their regimental publications, soldier-poets were also often genuinely light-hearted. On board the long train trip across Canada from Vancouver to the point of embarkation, Victoria's Charles Armstrong continued to edit and produce the 67th Battalion's newsletter, *The Western Scot.* He described the greatest trial of the rail journey as follows:

> A single distressing feature is recorded of the journey. About this time [1916], an order came out prohibiting the shaving of the upper lip, which is to say that the moustache was to be cultivated. A few were in desperation through the tardiness of the growth, while one sad wight set his impatience to rhyme, part of his apostrophe running as follows:—

> *Your King and Country need you*
> *And I think you ought to grow,*
> *But in spite of salves and tonics,*
> *Your growth is very slow.*

(*Western Scot Commemorative Edition,* 1917, 10)

The poem is evidence of the physical immaturity of soldiers from Victoria. As elsewhere, many were literally boys.

Needless to say, much worse trials were to follow once the soldier-poets arrived in Europe. Describing the daily lives of Canadian soldiers in the trenches, Desmond Morton writes that they "lived like tramps—filthy, lousy, sleeping rough in all weathers, usually hungry, and almost always fearful of what lay ahead."[3] Now, more than ever, sense of humor was necessary.

British and Canadian soldiers were much given to parody, as in *The Wipers Times*. Of course, these publications were not simply desperate efforts at morale-boosting, for amusing things must have happened in the trenches from time to time. At home, Victoria's readers could find much parody, satire, and plain good-humored verse composed by servicemen. "The Little Wet Home in the Trench" was written by a soldier who left Victoria with the 30th Overseas Battalion, then sent the poem to a resident here. It is a parody on "The Little Grey Home in the West", a 1911 song which was popular during the war. The last verses express the real unhappiness only partly concealed in the previous stanzas.

> *In my little wet home in the trench,*
> *That's the place where we fight with the French,*
> *The Germans all know*
> *So we have to keep low.*
>
> *In my little wet home in the trench*
> *There's no one to visit us there.*
> *For the place is all muddy and bare . . .*
>
> .
>
> *If only the war was to cease*
> *At the sound of the little word "Peace"*
> *With a fast beating heart*
> *I would willingly part*
> *With my little wet home in the trench.*

(*Colonist,* 1 October 1915, 5)

Despite—or perhaps because of—their miserable lives in the trenches, Canadians developed a reputation for ferocity, especially in their night-time raiding forays. No doubt they were frequently successful but, from one raid to the next, the experience was far from glorious, as one anonymous poet pointed out in his poem sent to the *Times*, "The Raid We Made on Fritz". I quote parts not noted above:

> *There were seven in our party,*
>   *The moon was shining bright.*
> *As we crawled out on our stomachs*
>   *Into "No Man's Land" that night . . .*
>
> *Next a shell dropped close beside me,*
>   *Lucky thing it was a "dud",*
> *But it left me lying gasping*
>   *With my throat choked up with mud.*
>
> *Then a "star-shell" floated upward,*
>   *Making it as bright as day,*
> *With the whole bunch lying on me*
>   *Covered in the mud I lay . . .*

(*Times*, 24 December 1917, 17) The poet claims that this was actually an easy foray and led to the capture of several Germans; indeed, he and his buddies "do it every day". The slight tone of sarcasm and the jaded realism of these verses is unusual. The works by soldier-poets published in the *Times* and the *Colonist* rarely alluded—even humorously—to these "negative" feelings, although the *Times* was more willing than the *Colonist* to print verses which undermined the romantic view of military service—even after Ottawa's censorship came into effect in 1915. [Fig.II.7.3]

Fig.II.7.3: "How'd That Happen, Chum—Shrapnel?"

Despite the mayhem and chaos of the trenches, some damage to equipment or uniforms had mundane causes. (*Canada in Khaki,* Vol. I, 75.)

8 **Fighting Fritz**

Apart from provoking healthy laughter, a sense of humor helped the soldier to forget temporarily that his job was to kill Germans—or at least to avoid violent death himself. If he remembered civilian attitudes in Victoria, we might assume that he regarded the enemy with implacable hatred. E.J. Down, chair of the local Victory Loan Committee, composed typical lyrics for a song which referred to the "ruthless Hun" (*Colonist,* 25 November 1917, 13). Ralph Younghusband, who was later to serve overseas, began his "Litany of the Trenches" with this self-righteous verse:

> *By the thunder of the guns*
> *And the cruelties of the Huns,*
> *On the weak, defenceless ones;*

Avenge our daughters and our sons!
Hear us, Holy Jesu!

(*Colonist,* 21 March 1917, editorial page)

Like Younghusband, Victoria's civilians felt a deep animosity to all things German, a mood which resulted in a riotous looting of businesses believed to belong to Germans in May 1915. In some cases, this attitude carried over into the trenches. Indeed, Charles Yale Harrison's protagonist describes Canadians fighting the Germans: "I am filled with a frenzied hatred for these men. They want to kill me but I will stay here and shoot at them until I am either shot or stabbed down. I grit my teeth. We are snarling, savage beasts."[1] [Fig.II.8.1]

The Bloody Huns?

Similarly, some of Victoria's soldiers began their service with "frenzied hatred". At the Willows Camp in Victoria, even after the European war had ended, poet and Rifleman Walter B. Ford referred to "the bloody Hun" (*Colonist,* 12 December 1918, editorial page). The experience of actual warfare, however, seem to have dulled local soldier-poets' quasi-religious anti-German fervor. Not a few probably sympathized with the feelings of Robert Service, expressed in one of his "Rhymes of a Red Cross Man", when he observed, "the dying Boche on the stretcher there has a queer resemblance to me."[2] Veterans and historians both have noted the lack of animosity towards the German enemy on the part of many Canadian and other Allied combatants.

Fig.II.8.1: "The Kind of a Foe We Fight"

Victoria civilians were encouraged to imagine the typical German soldier as a ruthless thug, oblivious to British "fair play", while the average Canadian soldier was an innocent, defenceless youth. The "Canuck"'s experience was often different and more nuanced. (*Victoria Daily Colonist,* 2 November 1918, 4.)

Memoirists and diarists refer to the Germans mainly as "Fritz", and uses the pronoun "he" or "him" acknowledging the enemy as a distinct human being. Similarly, Victoria's soldier-poets use this semi-affectionate nickname more frequently than they do the loaded term, "the Hun", probably because they knew that "Fritz" was in exactly the same miserable position as the "Tommy" or the "Canuck".

In battle, moreover, Canadians learned that the Germans were the best fighters in Europe. Perhaps for this reason, little vilification of the enemy soldier is found in the verse of Victoria's servicemen—unlike what is found in Victoria's civilian poetry. Did Victoria's editors exercise a prudent censorship? This is hard to know, but some local editors may have tried to limit the local "Hun"-bashing. An anonymous poem, originally from *Punch* and ostensibly by a soldier, was published in the *Colonist* (9 September 1915, 8) in which the poet admonished his patriotic, self-sacrificing mother: "Hating's not your style/Germans have mothers, too." The British poet-soldier Private Wilfrid J. Halliday, wrote "The Grave", which was printed in the *Times* (as usual, more daring than the *Colonist*), 16 June 1916, on its editorial page. The writer sees a young dead German, whom he describes as "innocent" and "sweet". No Victoria poet, however—civilian or military—went so far in print. [Fig.II.8.2]

Speaking of combatants generally, Modris Eksteins writes, "some men never lost their sense of romance and adventure".[3] Of the British Tommy, the veteran Charles E. Montague wrote of how he enjoyed "the mental peace, physical joy, the divinely simplified sense of having one clear aim, the remoteness from all the rest of the world."[4] Of Canadians, Desmond Morton agrees: "a few found their war experiences exhilarating."[5] What evidence does the poetry provide of Victoria soldiers' pleasure in combat?

Fig.II.8.2: "Some of Our Prisoners".

The soldier in the trenches had a more sophisticated view of the enemy. "Him of Hate" refers to the poem "Hymn of Hate", an anti-British diatribe written by Ernst Lissauer in 1913. "Zabern" refers to an incident in a town in German-occupied Alsace. Unrest there in 1913 was crushed by the German army in ways that were considered—by many Germans—to be arbitrary and illegal. (*Canada in Khaki*, Vol. 1, 53.)

I have found only one poem by a local poet which does so. Ralf Sheldon-Williams, serving with the Canadian Machine Gun Corps, wrote of soldiers having been "granted the privilege of taking part" in the war. Of the "Hundred Days", the last Canadian campaign in the war, which helped to drive the Germans to defeat, he wrote,

> Ah! But it was good to live through
> That Century of Dazzling suns, and good
> I think it must have been to die.[6]

Perhaps the University of British Columbia Librarian, John Ridington, was correct when he wrote that Canada's published war poets were "not so intent on the glory of the smashing blow, the delight in struggle and conquest, as on the sacrificial consecration of the spirit",[7] but I doubt that many of Victoria's soldier-poets were so spiritual in mood. Probably some local servicemen enjoyed aspects of the war; others hated all of it. Little of either extreme attitude appears in the published verse.

9 Our Funny Moods

Given their growing disillusionment with the nature of the war and the declining idealism which we have seen in the poetry of Victoria's soldiers, we may be surprised to read the statement of a local historian that "There was never a note of despondency in published letters".[1] As we know, any letter which expressed dissatisfaction with the progress of the war or the writer's own position in it would not likely to be published in Victoria or elsewhere in Canada, even if it passed the censor's scrutiny. Actually, letters (to be published or not) which officers read seem not, in fact, to have been particularly "despondent". Speaking of his fellow servicemen, Captain Robert Harvey of Victoria told the *Colonist* that "their letters are as cheery as can be" (11 April 1915,

16), which may have been true, given the fact that, even before his officer saw his correspondence, the soldier tended to self-censor what he wrote. "With few exceptions the letters are all the same, a dead level of dullness," commented veteran officer James Pedley, who also had to do the censoring. "The men talk of the weather and the food. They are always in the pink and hope their correspondent is the same and please send socks."[2] [Fig.II.9.1]

Fig.II.9.1: Happy Recruits.

A Canadian recruiting poster suggests that all volunteers were cheerful. Occasionally, Victoria soldiers' poetry suggested differently. (*Victoria Daily Times*, 29 October 1917, 11.)

On the other hand, myth-making may have been underway here. The notion that the Canadian soldier was stoic even when in pain was fostered by memoirists such as Charles Gordon, a Canadian Presbyterian padre, who remarked on "the uncomplaining endurance of our wounded". "Never once have I heard one single word of complaint—never one single word of regret for having come to the war—no single word of impatience."[3] Would a soldier—in agony from wounds or not—complain to an authority figure like a padre?

Nevertheless, most postwar memoirs continued to maintain that soldiers were usually content. In his chronicle of the First Canadian Division, Kenneth Radley writes, "Many Canadian regimental histories express a cheeriness . . . that never left those units."[4] More to the point, of the British forces in general, Canadian Sergeant William W. Murray claimed that the "spiritual distress" of poets such as Robert Graves or Siegfried Sassoon "was by no means characteristic of the men who took part [in the war] as a whole."[5] Although the memoirs of Will Bird and the novels of Peregrine Acland and Charles Yale Harrison (all veterans of the Canadian army) are critical of the way the war was fought, Canada had no Wilfred Owen.

Just a Bit Blue

Nevertheless, we must ask: do Victoria's soldier-poets mention "shell-shock" or damaging emotional trauma, what we now call post-traumatic stress disorder? Perhaps some would have agreed with Lieutenant Ralph Lewis of Nova Scotia, when he wrote later that "we never gave a thought to what we had gone through. A good thing, for if we did a few of us would be good patients for a lunatic asylum."[6] Such references to psychological distress in the published poetry, however, are rare. Of course, poets like Kenneth George Halley could call a battlefield "this hell" and have his work published on the *Colonist*'s editorial page (16 December 1916). In 1918, another poem of Halley's describes the "small grim-faced heaps" of the dead, "poor wrecks who lie too still to care" (*Colonist,* 13 March 1918, 10). But these remarks come across more as journalistic comments than an expression of shock or horror. Even so, the latter poem was published deep in the newspaper.

I have found at least one hint, however, of depression. In 1917, Private Edwin Freeman was recuperating from gassing at the Resthaven Hospital near Sidney where he found himself reliving in a poem the miseries of the trenches: "all this mud, this strife, this heat". Describing his fellow veterans, he refers to "all our funny moods". "Our nerves are anything but good", he wrote, adding that occasionally "you feel awful blue". Their "troubles" often make them "downhearted". Typically, the verses were buried on page twelve of the *Colonist* (28 January 1917). Descriptions of actual traumatic combat experiences are not mentioned. One suicidal poem, however, stands out. Cecil W. Tildesley, a Victoria artilleryman, composed the following "Verses at 3 a.m.", describing the dilemma of a "telephonist" trapped in an enemy attack. He concludes that living in hell would be preferable to his present situation:

> You grasp that good revolver—meant for such a pass as
> this—
> And point at your "window-of-the-soul",
> You press the giddy trigger—mechanics does the rest—
> And take up the peaceful job of shov'ling coal.

(*Times*, 10 October 1917, 16)

Perhaps because of the poet's tone of black humor and because the poem was published on page sixteen, the *Times'* editors, bolder than the *Colonist's*, thought the Chief Censor in Ottawa might not object.

A tone of a pessimism and despair also suffuses a poem by Charles Armstrong, who found a fallen and cracked bell in the ruins of a Belgian church. He imagined the bell speaking, lamenting the loss of "simple pleasures" swept away by "the common hurricane" and asking the poet,

> *To bury me*
> *Here in the debris of my chosen spot,*
> *That with familiar things I still may be,*
> *And, with familiar things, corrode—and rot!*

(*Canada in Khaki,* Vol. I, opp. 36)

Whereas Armstrong's poetry written before he arrived in France is "up-lifting", eager and humorous, his tone here is somber, for he had encountered the ravaging aspect of war. [Fig.II.9.1]

Clearly, the soldier-poets' descriptions of their psychological condition were limited by self-censorship or by the censorship of their officers or prospective editors. If their enthusiasm for the war lessened, still only a hint of discontent with the whole enterprise emerges in their verse. To be sure, many experienced homesickness, an emotion the expression of which apparently was allowed, although giving vent even to such a traditional and understandable feeling contradicted the soldiers' own self-image as tough warriors and might be considered bad for public morale.

One such poem did pass muster, perhaps because it expressed a generalized local patriotism. From a military hospital in England, Private Thomas A. Hollins of Victoria wrote verses expressing the notion that "the province of B.C., . . . [is] . . . where I long to be;" "Victoria is a shrine, both human and divine, with Esquimalt standing sentinel and guard . . ." (*Colonist,* 19 October 1918). Such

Fig.II.9.1: "The Fallen Bell"

This poem by Charles Armstrong, a Victoria journalist, indicates the sobering jolt which many volunteers experienced in France, a shock which could provoke depression. In his case, the poet was sent back to Canada with "heart trouble". (*Canada in Khaki,* Vol. 1, opp. 36.)

an expression of loyalty to the home province seems to have been an acceptable theme in poetry, and so we find this verse on the newspaper's editorial page. In 1917, after several months overseas, Victoria's George Jarvis was homesick and wrote in "Thoughts of Home", "We only wish this war would end/ So we could homeward roam".[7] These feelings were expressed in a private letter which Jarvis' officer apparently deemed acceptable. Gunner Ralf Sheldon-Williams wrote that "letters from home" "make us just a bit *blue*" [his emphasis]. Victoria newspaper readers, however, would not have read these latter two poems during the war because they were published later.[8] On the other hand, the *Colonist* published Ralph Younghusband's poignant lament for his friend, James Douglas Hodding, killed in action (1 April 1919, 12). (See below.) Similarly the *Semi-Weekly Tribune* (21 October 1918, 7) allowed its readers to sense how soldiers might experience grief when its editor printed an American's lament, "My Buddy's Gone" but such "un-manly" feelings were rarely published. Admiration of the character of fellow soldiers was expressed often, as in Vallie's "Ode to Joe" ("a clear, consistent player of the game") but typically the poet's grief is muted. (See above.)

In Bondage to Unjust Necessity

Robert Nichols described British soldiers as feeling that they were "in bondage to unjust necessity".[9] A few Canadians, for their part, seem to have developed such a pessimistic outlook. A Major in Princess Patricia's Canadian Light Infantry, Talbot Papineau, privately described his and his comrades' state of mind as a "black mood of hopelessness" in 1917.[10] Only slightly less darkly, Victoria's Charles Armstrong assumed the inevitability of his own death:

When I kick in—
Just think the best of me:
Think of the good things I had hoped to do,
Forgetting those I'd done were all too few,
Some part lives on. Just plant the rest of me,
When I kick in . . . .

(The Western Scot, July 1916, 19; reprinted in *The Western Scot. Commemorative Edition,* 1917, 43)

Because these verses were not published in one of Victoria's civilian newspapers or periodicals, but in the soldier's battalion newsletter, the civilian public was not likely to see them. Nevertheless, they suggest that, when a soldier had spent time in the trenches (as was the case with Armstrong), he could sense the futility of the ongoing war of attrition and the likelihood of his not surviving for much longer.

* * *

To summarize: the poetry of Victoria's soldiers reveals much about the values and attitudes of our great-grandparents a century ago. They went off to battle filled with illusions about the nature of modern warfare and with the desire to protect the British Empire from an "evil foe". Most poets were sure of an early, crushing victory over the Germans. Many did not feel explicitly Canadian in a modern sense but were proud to be British, and in fact often were so by birth and citizenship. Their poetic expression was in language that was high-flown and inappropriate. Yet most aspired to certain standards of male character and behavior. To a degree at least, after the "front experience", the content and language of their published verse changed. Food, alcohol and tobacco become themes crowding out high-minded ideals and confidence. A sense of humor was a saving attitude in irritating or desperate situations. However much some of them did so at the start of the war, Victoria's soldiers (unlike many civilian poets), did not usually regard the enemy as an evil monster.

Much of the foregoing applies to the lives and outlooks of other Canadian soldiers, not just those from Victoria. This study of the city's soldier-poets, however, raises some questions about their and our own view of the Great War. For example, was the Battle of Vimy Ridge as important in raising the pride of the Canadian soldier as we have been taught to believe? The poetry does not suggest so. Was comradeship in the trenches so vital to the soldier's well-being as we have always assumed? Again, Victoria's military poets give little evidence of this. Yet these two themes must have appealed to editors who would have been happy to publish verse which expounded them. Are they postwar myths?

Before we consider this possibility, a brief digression is in order.

10 The Siberian Muddle

After the fall of Russia's liberal government to the Bolsheviks in October 1917 and the Treaty of Brest-Litovsk (March 1918, in which Lenin's government ceded much territory to Germany), the western Allies feared that the still-belligerent Germans would establish submarine ports in Siberia. Moreover, ideologically they were opposed to everything that the new Marxist government stood for. In late 1918, the Canadian government, therefore, in tandem with its allies, sent soldiers to unseat the Bolsheviks. Enthusiasm for soldiering had waned and most conscripts did not want to leave Canada. Nor, for that matter, did most Canadian civilians want their "boys" crusading in foreign lands again so soon after the carnage in western Europe. Those servicemen who sent to suppress the Communists, however, produced a very small crop of works which rehearse the idealism and enthusiastic warrior mood which had lasted, in some few cases, beyond the end of the Great War. The vocabulary and the imagery was the same as we saw in the early poems of Victoria's volunteers. While use of "high diction" and commitment to a crusade had dwindled in the C.E.F. in France and Flanders, some of it still flickered in the verse of those going to Siberia.

Despite having heard of or experienced the horrors of the European war on the western front, a few Canadians were happy to serve in Canada's attempt both to outflank the Germans and to put down the Marxist Revolution. With the developing "red scare", they were able to transfer their anger at the Germans to the new Russian leaders. Rifleman Walter B. Ford, training at the Willows Camp, believed that Canadians were naïve about the continued danger of "the bloody Hun" because

> . . . the Kaiser in his castle, just across the Holland line
> Wirelesses the Bolsheviki "Ach, my boys, you're doing
> fine!"

Obviously, Ford had some of the optimism and enthusiasm of a 1914 volunteer. In his verses entitled "The Siberians Will Stick", he vowed that he and his colleagues would "play the game". No doubt hearing about disaffection in the ranks of the "Siberians", Ford wrote,

> Now and then a weak-kneed quitter, freedom by desertion
> seeks,

> *But the line is holding steady—yellow only shows in streaks.*

(*Colonist,* 12 December 1918, editorial page)

Similarly, Ralph Younghusband wrote from "Russian Island Vladivostok, Siberia" that he had heard "the soul of Russia breathing forth a prayer/for liberty from out a heart of care" (*Colonist,* 1 April 1919, 12).

Ultimately five thousand Canadians troops were sent to Vladivostok in eastern Siberia, and a smaller group to northern Russia near Archangel and Murmansk. They included two infantry battalions, some field artillery, and machine gunners. By late 1918, over four thousand men—mainly conscripts—had been assembled at the Willows Camp in Victoria, prior to embarking for Siberia. Public opinion opposed sending these men to Russia. Some Canadians pointed out that, as draftees, their purpose was only for the defence of Canada. Labor leaders and some Members of Parliament disapproved of sending them, apparently to interfere in a foreign country's political life. In Victoria, "the Siberians" had specific grievances as well. The fall of 1918 was unusually wet—a fact which, as we know, Rifleman Shepherd lamented ("Does it always, always rain?"). (Fig. II.7.2) The Spanish flu had arrived and quarantine was established. Morale sank and discontent arose. The majority opposed going to Siberia and insubordination was common. One unit, the 259th Battalion (Canadian Rifles), formed in September 1918, consisted of 1083 troops, of which only 378 had enlisted voluntarily. As they were marching to board their ship in Victoria on 21 December 1918, some of them mutinied on Fort Street. Ultimately, all the men were herded aboard at bayonet-point.[1] Later, on 31 March 1919 a section of the Canadian Field Brigade in northern Russia also refused to obey orders.

For his part, Rifleman Ford enthusiastically had predicted that "we'll smite the Bolsheviki if they give us half a chance" (*Colonist,* 12 December 1918, editorial page). The experience of the Canadians in Russia, however, was no more inspiring than that of their comrades in Western Europe. Signaller Earl Marling, a volunteer previously employed in the circulation department of the *Colonist*, was with the Canadian Field Artillery in northern Russia. When this unit lost their identity as they were merged with the British force, Marling sent verses to his mother in Victoria in which he imagined, at a military review, General Currie asking Prime Minister Robert Borden what became of these Canadians. "Sir Robert then replied: 'Of them I never thought.' That brigade, unfortunately we have forgot" (*Colonist,* 10 June 1919, 8).

By the end of December 1918, Borden had decided to withdraw these "forgotten brigades" back home. Withdrawal began in April 1919 and on June 20, 1919, the last Canadians arrived in Victoria from Siberia. "The Siberian muddle"[2] had ended. The expedition, confusedly planned and executed, was a failure. For our purposes, however, it serves as a reminder of the idealism and enthusiasm for a foreign crusade which still prevailed among some Victoria poets, even in 1919.

11 Myths and Mysteries

Many of Victoria's soldiers—as represented by their poet comrades—went to war in 1914 with a deluded view of what modern war was all about. Moreover, they had the notion that the

British Empire was the pinnacle of moral and political civilization, a view which most Canadians would not entertain today. The experience of trench combat brought the soldier-poets closer to reality, a fact reflected in their verse. They were disillusioned about the nobility of warfare, and began to lose interest in the Empire as a cause. They became more concerned to describe the food, the rum, the tobacco and the absurd incidents which occurred in training or in the trenches on the Western Front. They revelled in humor and avoided (and were compelled to avoid) descriptions which would upset civilians at home. With the possible exception of their greater difficulty in abandoning British loyalties, local soldiers' experience was probably not very different from that of men from other parts of Canada. Their personal values were similar, too.

On the other hand, however, if we look in this poetry for some of the mention of incidents, feelings and attitudes which we have come to automatically associate with the phrase "First World War", we look almost in vain.[1] Few Victoria poets, for example, mention the German gas attacks of 1915 or the later use of gas by both sides. Although one would expect them not to go into the grisly detail of Wilfred Owen's "Dulce Et Decorum Est", why did only one Victoria poet (Kenneth G. Halley) refer to these events? Several popularly held beliefs about the Great War are revealed as possibly having little foundation in fact.

Angry Veterans?

Victoria's soldier-poets, as we have seen, do not seem to have been "bewildered" as to their own definition of male virtues. They knew who they were and what was expected of them as soldiers. More important, the published verse of Victoria's soldiers during and shortly after the war does not present a picture of disillusioned and bitter veterans of the Great War. Of course, the fact that the ranks of Victoria's servicemen produced no brilliant Wilfred Owen, no angry Charles Yale Harrison and no embittered Erich Maria Remarque does not mean that there were no angry veterans returning to Victoria in 1919. Censorship, editorial selection and their own reticence inhibited expression of their feelings. Yet what we have seen suggests that better poetry, more successful novels and many movies not withstanding, the existence of an embittered Great War soldier—at least in Victoria—may be a myth.

Living on the Edge of the Wilderness?

On the other hand, at least one widespread misconception— especially in Europe—about Canada's servicemen is supported by their published poetry. Victoria's soldier-poets themselves contributed to the image of the "typical" Canadian soldier as a rugged pioneer outdoorsman. Perhaps Robert Service, who had lived in Victoria and the Cowichan Valley c. 1896-1904, began this tradition in his "The Man From Athabaska", a description of a sixty-year-old backwoodsman, trapper and fisherman who readily volunteers in 1914.[2] Fifty years later, Pierre Berton buttressed the misconception, writing that, "To a very large extent the men who fought at Vimy had worked on farms and lived on the edge of the wilderness."[3] [Fig.II.11.1]

Victoria's Sergeant Gould praised his 102nd battalion because they were "not drawn from city clerks", but from farmers, loggers, mill workers and miners "who have the wit to live in open spaces, free from care" [sic] (Colonist, 16 January 1916, 5). Some truth adheres to this description of the 102nd, although one doubts that

Fig.II.11.1: "How Klondyke Bill Joined Up. According to
the Artists and According to Fact"

This cartoon suggests that some soldiers were aware that a false image
of the typical Canadian recruit had been created by poets such as Robert
Service and certain Victoria writers. (*Canada in Khaki*, Vol. II, 74.)

living in "open spaces" provided freedom from care! Similarly, Lieutenant-Colonel Ross described his 67th Battalion (the Western Scots who trained in Victoria) as follows:

> They have hunted the bear in his darkest lair,
> And tracked through the woods and snows;
> Through the heat and rain they have ridden the plain,
> In the south where the Kootenay flows.

(*The Western Scot,* 2 February 1916, 9)

This may have been true because both the 67th and 102nd Battalions drew men from northern British Columbia.

The majority of Canadian soldiers, however, were unskilled, skilled, or clerical workers who hailed from cities. 64.8% of Canadian soldiers were factory laborers. 18.5% were from clerical occupations, while white collar workers outnumbered farmers.[4] They may have been fans of outdoor sports, but few were brawny "he-men", much less experienced athletes. However, in Britain the unfortunate behavior of some members of the First Contingent on Salisbury Plain in 1914-15 helped to create the image of the Canadian as a rough and drunken brawler with fighting abilities inbred by the hostile Canadian climate. Furthermore, the use of native Canadians as snipers led to their reputation as efficient killers and helped to support the image of the Canadian soldier as an instinctive warrior.

Camaraderie?

Supporting and caring for their buddies was also part of the soldier's concept of honor. This comradeship in wartime entails a sense of responsibility toward and dependence on other soldiers and the resulting sense of fellowship. It was and is vital to the emotional and physical survival of all servicemen—and now—women. Not even their loved ones at home could inspire the loyalty and courage implicit this bond. Increasingly, as the Great War dragged on, many of our great-grandfathers fought, not for the Empire or for the Belgians, but for their friends. At least this picture of trench loyalty is the received wisdom which most Canadians entertain and, in many cases, may be a true image.

Local soldier-poets, however, make little mention of the camaraderie of the trenches. Not that the theme is totally absent. In Cowichan, Ralph Younghusband wrote: "Somewhere in France, dear comrade, you are lying/ Beneath a wooden cross . . ." (*Colonist,* 1 April 1919, 12). Other expressions of such love are rare. A similar poem appeared in the *Semi-Weekly Tribune* (21 October 1918, 7), written by an American writer lamenting the death of "my Buddy". Given the later prevalence of the "comradeship" notion, editors might have been expected to have published more of verse on the subject, if only to reassure Victoria's civilian readers that their men had some emotional support at the front. But there was little published on this theme.

Did Canada's soldiers experience less comradeship in the trenches than we have been led to believe? Or were Victoria's servicemen in particular less prone to the experience? Generalizations, of course, are dangerous. I note, however, that the Canadian soldiers James Pedley and Will Bird had their belongings stolen from them—by other Canadian soldiers.[5] The instances of desertion and crime—even of execution by firing squad—suggest that there were some men at least who felt no loyalty to their comrades. We might entertain the notion that the camaraderie of the trenches was a product of the wistful fantasy of veterans' postwar recollections, men who felt out of step with and neglected by uncomprehending civilians and an ungenerous government. We should at least consider the point of view of novelist Charles Yale Harrison's protagonist:

> Camaraderie—esprit de corps—good fellowship—
> these are words for journalists to use, not for us. Here
> in the line they do not exist. We fight among ourselves.[6]

A harsh view, perhaps, but how can one explain the absence in the verse of Victoria's soldier-poets of a theme which several generations have come to assume was the only redeeming feature of trench life?

Marching to Calvary?

Some civilian poets liked to present the Canadian soldier as a Christ-like figure. Marjorie Pickthall, for example, wrote about "Marching Men":

> Under the level winter sky
> I saw a thousand Christs go by.
> They sang an idle song and free
> As they went up to calvary.[7]

For Canada's churches, writes Thomas P. Socknat, the Great War became "an apocalyptic crusade, an eschatological confrontation between good and evil, between Christianity and the Antichrist epitomized by Germany."[8] Even some of the first soldier-poets, as we have seen, thought of themselves as "fighting for the good" and for Christian values. The ostensibly dogged faith of the soldier was emphasized by the British poet, W.H. Littlejohn, in "Holy Communion, Suvla Bay" which described a battlefront service in the Dardanelles, attended by devout soldiers (*Colonist,* 11 June 1918, editorial page). Although not written by a local poet, such verse gave a comforting impression to Victoria's readers: the cause was sacred and their men were God-fearing knights.

On the other hand, the local soldiers make little explicit reference to Christian faith in their poems. They were, perhaps, like the "Tommy", who "folded up his religion in 1914, and put it away, as it were, in a drawer with his other civil attire to wait until public affairs should again permit of their use."[9] Clearly, if any soldier-poet submitted to a Victoria editor a poem critical of the Christian interpretation of the war, it would not have been published. The absence of such verse, however, may also be a reflection of the soldiers' own growing skepticism about organized religion. Possibly Victoria's soldiers felt as Will Bird's friend who, "like the majority, . . . strongly resented being made to fall in a parade and go and listen to the padres and officers sing 'Fight the Good Fight' and a sermon he scorned."[10]

Canada's Coming of Age?

Mark Zuehlke writes that the Battle of Vimy Ridge "was Canada's proudest moment of the war and one that came to symbolize its emergence from colony to nation."[11] Canadians have been told repeatedly that Vimy was a distinct milestone at which the country "came of age" and that national self-awareness was born out of that slaughter. Certainly, during the war, Victoria's soldiers began to express less reverence for the British imperial connection. But as we have seen, little Canadian patriotism appears in the verse.

An incident in Charles Yale Harrison's autobiographical novel, *Generals Die in Bed,* suggests that at least one soldier felt no sense of distinct "Canadian-ness". A general speaks to the men about

> the greater glory of Canadian arms. The term "Canadian arms" sound strange to us. Most of us are clerks, students, farmers and mechanics—but staff officers have a way of speaking like that. To us this business of military glory and arms means carrying parties, wiring fatigues, wet clothes and cowering in a trench under shell-fire.[12]

Possibly Harrison's view, expressed publicly in 1928, is the jaded recollection of a disillusioned individual. On the other hand, in 1919 the U.B.C. Librarian, believed that

> Nationalism is passing away . . . Patriotism in its old sense—that of love for a geographical locality or historical sequence of events—had been gradually dying as a motive stimulus to men.[13]

Today we might dismiss this view as "wishful thinking". However, Sheldon-Williams, who relished his military experience, wrote verses which may support Ridington's view of at least some Canadian soldiers' attitude. Of his comrades, he wrote

> They didn't pull off any grand-stand play:
> They seldom did much in the gallery way;
> They were generally dirty and sometimes shaved,
> But—never the flag of their country waved.[14]

It seems possible, at any rate, that the great upsurge in Canadian national pride which journalists and patriots date to the year 1917 is an invention of the post-war era. This theory is buttressed by at least one recent study of post-war myth-making.[15]

With one exception, neither the *Times* nor the *Colonist* published any poems by local soldier-poets which mention the Battle of Vimy Ridge. Only Charles Armstrong, writing about the "first draft" (the volunteers of August 1914) declared:

> *Each took toll of their slim numbers*
> *   (Nought their courage could abridge),*
> *And it flamed amid the thunders,*
> *   On the heights of Vimy Ridge.*

(*Times, 28* August 1917, 15)

The *Times* did publish a long poem, "The Charge of the Canadians at Vimy Ridge" by John Hooper, identified as "Winnipeg, late Royal School of Gunnery and N.C. Officer N.W. Field Force". Part of it reads,

> *Canadians, charge! Not one of them shrank*
> *As their sharp full cheer from rank on rank*
> *Rose joyously with a willing breath,—*
> *Rose as a greeting hail to death,*
> *Forward, the Canadians,—across the bridge,—*
> *Forward, the Canadians, take Vimy Ridge . . .*

(*Times,* 24 October 1917, 8)

The *Times* presented Hooper's three verses in a frame,[16] but Hooper was not a local poet. If the Battle of Vimy Ridge had in fact made a great impression on Victoria's soldier-poets, the patriotic newspaper reader (newly aware of his/her nationhood) would expect to read some poetic commemoration of the event on its first anniversary in 1918. Editors would have been sure to welcome such verse, particularly from soldiers. But neither civilian nor military poets hailing from Victoria seem to have been impressed enough to memorialize it.

Judging by the evidence of Victoria's soldier-poets, therefore, whereas some Canadian soldiers may have come from outdoor professions, inured to physical danger and hardship, during the war they do not seem to have been especially conscious of the value of camaraderie and they were not religious in any orthodox sense. They were not bitter or angry about their experience of war and their Canadian patriotism was muted.

12 Censorship and Reality

In their poems, as in their letters home, most soldiers did not usually write about picking lice off their bodies, avoiding marauding rats, stepping over rotting corpses, dealing with "trench foot", collecting the body parts of killed friends—conditions which could cause more than "the blues". [Fig.II.12.1] The subject of truth versus official and self-censorship has been a theme throughout this study. I have maintained that these poems offer twenty-first century Canadians a glimpse into the mindset of their ancestors a hundred years ago, especially for the year 1914 in which they went off to war. As we read these poems, however, the question arises: do they reveal the whole truth about the soldier-poet's experiences? Obviously, some servicemen had an easier time in Europe than did others. And, to be sure, the values of most of Victoria's servicemen are probably revealed clearly enough in this verse—and give us cause to reflect on our own attitudes today. But what about the Canauck's day-to-day experience—the "nitty-gritty"? It is likely that the poems do not reveal much. But why not?

Fig.II.12.1: "The Canuck"

In this sketch, the Canadian soldier's wirecutter seems to be of more use to him than his rifle, although his bayonet appears to have been used. Such realism only rarely made it past the various walls of censorship applied to poetic or graphic descriptions of trench warfare. Compare his image with that of the "knight-in-shining-armor". (*Canada in Khaki*, Vol. I, 43.)

From their verse we know that their view of war and of the Empire, for example, changed over time. We know, as well, however, that, to avoid upsetting their loved ones, the men themselves refrained in their letters home from describing their most horrific experiences or complaining about their miseries. If they were too explicit, of course, their officers would censor their letters. The same phenomenon seems to have occurred in the verse which they sent to Victoria's editors. As well, it seems likely that, in any submitted poetry, they proudly refused to admit any disillusionment or unhappiness. In their own publications, they strove to keep up their fellows' morale by jokes and bravado. One has to read between the lines to sense the effort made here to suppress "negative" feelings. These newsletters did not usually reach civilian readers, but their tone is similar to verse and prose that did.

In the trenches, between themselves, they seem to have been franker about their opinions, if not their fears. Will Bird remembered that his comrades gave vent to "long and bitter denunciations of the folly of [the Battle of] Passchendaele."[1] The same slaughter of 1917 left one Canadian lieutenant dumbstruck. "I cannot begin to describe the awfulness of war and wouldn't if I could."[2] On the other hand, little of this openness appears in the poetry of Victoria's volunteers. Instead, our great-grandfathers did as their counterparts in the armies of other belligerents did. They tried mightily to avoid "beefing", criticizing their leaders, or expressing any depression. In 1917 the *Times* published a poem entitled tellingly "Keep Smiling" by an anonymous British prisoner of war in Germany. Two verses read:

> *Better the world with your gladness,*
> *Smile at the "barbed wires" of life,*

> *Laugh and be glad that there's someone awaits you,*
> *P'r'haps mother, sweetheart, or wife.*

(Times, 22 October 1917, editorial page)

No doubt this attitude was also maintained in the trenches and probably succeeded in most cases much of the time.

Consequences of Self-Censorship

Soldiers did not want to upset their wives, parents, children or sweethearts with graphic description of grisly events. Unfortunately, this sort of self-censorship contributed to some civilians' later failure to understand their husbands' and fathers' experience and feelings. The *Colonist* helped to perpetrate this impression when it published a poem by "A.S. Barton of Victoria", presumably a civilian (12 February 1916, 5) in which he praised the "cheery song and joke and toast" which the poet maintained characterized life in the trenches. (Fig. II.9.1) The *Colonist* concluded that "the Canadian soldiers are in the best of spirits". We might even assume that Victoria's soldiers felt compelled to maintain alertness on both the European front—where their lives depended on vigilance—and on the home front—where the feelings of their relatives needed to be protected.

An equally powerful motive for self-censorship was the soldier's desire to maintain the image he had cultivated while going off to war—that of the manly, courageous, and uncomplaining warrior "hero". If he complained about military life, he may have felt embarrassed by reminders of his early enthusiasm for the war. And so he maintained the proverbial "stiff upper lip". After all, volunteers had responded to the call for "men of grit" and "men with hearts of oak"—as in Leonard McLeod Gould's "Call to the

102nd Battalion" (*Colonist*, 16 January 1916, 5). Were they now going to admit that they lacked grit or oaken hearts?

Official Censorship

Soldiers knew that their officers kept watch on the mail they sent home. Victoria officers (and poets) Armstrong and Harvey, for example, both spent many hours censoring their men's correspondence. For obvious and justifiable reasons, officers could block out or remove any facts about troop movements, armaments, places—and morale—which soldiers mentioned in their letters. The men were not supposed to seal their letters before their company officers read them. They had to use "Somewhere in France" as the return address on their letters or postcards. The latter were used by some less literate soldiers, with the ticking off the lines on a printed form: such as "I am quite well". But even the composed letters are short and not especially personal. The truth about military disasters such as the Battle of the Somme, therefore, never reached the reading public in Victoria.

Moreover, if a soldier-poet wrote something to be published in a local journal, his work was also censored by civilian authorities. The editors of local newspapers and periodicals were subject to the surveillance of the Chief Censor in Ottawa, who encouraged them to print only the most uplifting descriptions of the war. In the War Measures Act of 22 August 1914, Clause 6 provided for "censorship and control and suppression of publications, writing, maps, plans, photographs, communications and means of communication". As well, the Act allowed for the appointment of "Chief Press Censor". Accordingly, in June 1915 Lieutenant-Colonel (and historian) Ernest J. Chambers took office and began to spread idealized reports about battles to newspapers and other media so that readers

could not know about the repeated failures to break through
the German lines. He was empowered to act against people who
criticized military policy, causing public disaffection or possibly
aiding the enemy. Because such accounts might hinder recruitment,
reports of casualties were not to mention the fact that sometimes
entire units were slaughtered. Chambers told journalists at the
front to stress the courage of Canada's victorious soldiers and to
downplay the war's unpleasantness. In London, Max Aitken, in
charge of the Canadian War Records Office, screened all stories
related to his homeland. He made sure than Canadian heroism
was emphasized and "Hun barbarism" was stressed. Aitken's
publication, *Canada in Khaki* (two volumes 1917), emphasized
good humor and optimism. The first volume of this periodical, for
example, included a full page collage of thirteen photo-portraits of
Canadian soldiers, all smiling broadly. The caption reads, "There is
no such thing as a gloomy Canadian soldier. These snapshots taken
in the front line should convert the worst pessimist."[3]

Given these facts, both popular and academic historians have
maintained that the Canadian civilian reader did not know the worst
about conditions on the Western Front. Pierre Berton maintained
that "the brutal truth never got through", because Canadians were
"lulled by a false picture of a struggle in which their clean-limbed,
courageous boys, heroes all, fought against a black-hearted and
beastly enemy."[4] Concurring, Jeffrey Keshen maintains that
Canadian civilians lived in a "cocoon-like environment".[5] The
result, according to Robert Nichols, was that "the civilian was still
in much the same condition of ignorance and innocent romanticism
that had characterized himself [the soldier] in 1914."[6] The belief
that men at the front were always light-hearted was sustained by
Victoria's soldier-poets themselves, especially in the humorous

verse that they wrote in or sent back to that city. As we know, by 1918 Victoria readers would not have had a chance yet to read much, if any, of the bitterly critical and disillusioned works of the British "war poets". Even if they were somehow known, none of their works would have been considered suitable for publication in Victoria during the conflict.

Sights that Beggar Description

One Canadian soldier wrote in his diary, "the sights that met our gaze were so horrible and ghastly that they beggar description."[7] As noted earlier, the literary language of the nineteenth century was inadequate to describe the sights, sounds and smells of the trenches on the Western front. "Cultural codes of literary decorum," writes J.M. Winter, "precluded unexpurgated accounts of profanity and horror."[8] If their friends died by violent dismemberment or suffered a slow, agonizing death by disemboweling, both of which were common in the Great War, soldier-poets did not refer to it in their works.

As we have seen, resignation and a stoic endurance prevailed. Occasionally a soldier might allow himself the expression of melancholy, genteely expressed, or—even more rarely—a description of homesickness—and, as we have seen, his officer and a later editor might allow this to pass.

Euphemisms

In fact, the soldier-poets rarely refer to dying or death in any explicit way. This was partly because, in nineteenth century literature, death became an almost beautiful event, a journey from a life of care to one of peace. In this vein, Victoria's Lieutenant-Colonel Lorne Ross described a dead soldier as "resting in peace", and "slumbering".[9] "Quite a few of the boys are gone across the Great

Divide" wrote one soldier to his mother.[10] Charles Armstrong foresaw his own death as simply, "When I Kick In" (incorrectly as it turned out). "R.F.L.", a soldier-poet recuperating at Victoria's Royal Jubilee Hospital, referred in a poem to his "pals, . . . Gone West to the Great Unseen" (Colonist, 16 February 1919, 9). Captain Halley suggested that the corpses in "no-man's land" were merely sleeping "in never-ending rest"(*Colonist, 13* March 1918, 10).

Despite censorship and euphemisms, however, Victoria's readers could soon understand that this "great" war was not like any other in which Canada had been involved. It was much worse than any romantic account of warfare described and possibly much worse than the official reports revealed. This is the view of Ian Hugh Maclean Miller who holds that historians such as Berton exaggerate, maintaining that, in Toronto at least, citizens were not ignorant of the conditions in the trenches. No "massive conspiracy to manipulate the public into supporting a war they knew was wrong" existed.[11] For his part, in a study of three diverse Canadian cities, Robert Allen Rutherdale takes the middle road. While acknowledging that newspapers provided "distorting mirrors, misleading settings, and illusionary situations", he maintains that "few Canadians were isolated entirely from the war's carnage."[12] As far as Victoria is concerned, Rutherdale's view applies, because, despite the prevalence of "high diction" and a deluded understanding of the nature of the war, Victoria's readers could occasionally sense in some of the published verse the fact that all was not well with "the boys" in Flanders and northern France.

Exceptions

Loopholes in the operation of censorship existed with the result that Victoria civilians, although trying to cling to a romanticized image of warfare, learned something about the miseries of trench life and the unhappiness of their soldiers. Even when the soldier-poet affirmed the war's purpose and his own and his comrades' resolve (as all did), Victoria's readers could not fail to know that this war was a ghastly and un-glorious business. A very long poem by the American Sayers Coe, entitled "The Dark Hour", in which a soldier fearfully anticipates a dawn attack, includes the lines,

> *The night is past,*
> *And life begins anew,*
> *For us the dawn held promise*
> *Of fear and pain and death,*
> *Of straining lungs and bursting heart,*
> *Of maddened cries from blood-crazed brains,*
> *Of raging tumult—*
> *And eternal peace.*

(*Colonist,* 30 September 1917, 20)

This vivid description of a soldier's terrors appeared in the feature "Men, Women and Events", offered by the *Colonist*'s "women's editor" Nora Bertrand de Lugrin, daughter of the newspaper's editor-in-chief, Charles Bertrand de Lugrin. Similarly, although another poet's verses were published (presumably) safely on page seven of the *Times*, he described how soldiers' "limbs were torn and shattered/By German shot and shell" (*Times,* 4 August 1917, 7). The local soldier-poet Ralph Younghusband told *Colonist* readers about "this dreadful slaughter" (21 March 1917, editorial page). In an otherwise serene appreciation of his treatment at Resthaven, Edwin Freeman recalled the trenches: "this mud, this strife, this heat" (*Colonist,* 28 January 1917, 12). In an unusually vivid description of trench warfare, Lieutenant Halley wrote

"Afterwards" in which something of the numbing exhaustion of trench combat is evident.

> *... High above a brilliant rocket soars,*
> *And down between the lines the barrage roars.*
>
> *Gone is the silence—nerve destroying screams*
> *Herald the shells which hurtle thro' the air;*
> *Columns of mud spout up in fan-shaped streams,*
> *Splinters of steel are shrieking everywhere,*
> *While powder smoke, a reeking, dusky pall,*
> *Falls like a great drop curtain over all.*
>
> *Thro' the dense fog the rifle bullets whine;*
> *Rattling machine guns hurl their leaden rain:*
> *Wave after wave breaks on the thinning line,*
> *Rolling away to form and charge again,*
> *While thro' this hellish music loudly runs*
> *The never ending thunder of the guns.*
>
> *Crowded and close the wavering advance*
> *Crouches to burst of shrapnel overhead.*
> *Down thro' their ranks the high explosives dance.*
> *Hell's imps and outcasts dancing for the dead,*
> *All wreathed in smoke that ghoulish ballet there,*
> *Mocks these poor wrecks who lie too still to care ....*

(*Colonist,* 13 March 1918, 10)

Ernst Jünger, a German soldier, wrote about how, after the Battle of Passchendaele, "chivalry . . . took a final farewell".[13] Canadian soldiers certainly knew this and expressed their awareness in their own publications. In 1916 Charles Armstrong presented a realistic image of the deceptively charming French countryside in a poem published in the 67th Battalion's newsletter. In an unusual blast of realism, he described "The Sniper" hiding "All through the pleasant summer day" beneath a tree. Suddenly he spies his prey and, in cold-blooded fashion,

> . . . *his body stretches, straight and tall—*
> *A loud report, quick flash of flame,*
> *And there behind yon distant sand-bag wall*
> *A lad goes down who'll never rise again.*

(*The Western Scot,* 24 May 1916; *Commemorative Edition,* [1917] 17)

No dashing élan was experienced by "A Soldier in the Trenches" who sent a poem to the *Times* (24 December 1917, 17), in which he described a "raid we made on Fritz". As we have seen, he gashed himself with his own bayonet, then was kicked by his sergeant, "right behind the ear." At the very least, Victoria's civilian readers could know that the war was messy, bloody and unglorious.

Unfortunately for the veterans, censorship and reticence made their adjustment to postwar civilian life more difficult. On the reaction of British civilians to hearing about some of the horrifying events in the trenches, Robert Nichols imagined civilians responding, "No, it couldn't be as bad as all that. Aren't you exaggerating? Surely your experience was exceptional. One mustn't harp on the dark side of things . . ."[14] Jeffrey Keshen agrees, adding that later "civilians grew impatient with Canadians returning from overseas who could not promptly re-adapt and thrive by displaying those manly qualities, that . . . had brought a succession of stupendous victories and glory to the country."[15] Desmond Morton and Glenn Wright have described how "winning the second battle" (returning to civilian life) was so challenging for many Canadian Great War veterans.[16] Ironically, the content and tone of soldier's own verse was partly responsible for civilians' unsympathetic reaction to veterans' problems.

13 Carry On!

The plethora of novels, books, articles, films and television programs on the Great War suggests that it remains a wound in the psyche of Western civilization. In Victoria, BC, as in the rest of Canada, November 11 is still commemorated as "Remembrance Day" often with the armistice of 1918 taking precedence over events of 1939-1945. For many young people, however, our fascination with First "Great" War of the 20th century may seem puzzling, especially when they read the letters and poetry of local soldiers. Why were so many local men willing to die for an empire which seems now so manifestly unjust and racist? Why did not the put-upon Canucks mutiny en masse (as did many French and Russians)? Why did young men have such deluded notions about war and where did they learn to write about "glorious crusades" in the way they did? Why did they not tell the truth about military service on the Western Front?

"I can't see any daylight as to when this damn war will end . . .", wrote one Canadian soldier. By enlisting, however, he believed that he "did the right thing . . . whether the war was wrong or not does not alter that fact."[1] No doubt he was also determined to "carry on" until it was over. A typical work of art, "Painted Expressly for the *Colonist*" in 1917, showed a classically robed female figure standing behind a Canadian soldier who looks into the distance. Her outstretched hand seems to indicate the tenor of the caption which reads "Canada, Carry On!" (5 August, 13). John McCrae's famous "In Flanders Fields", far from being a lament over years of slaughter, urges Allied soldiers to "take up our quarrel with the foe" (*Colonist,* 26 October 1918, 4). The *Times* published a poem, ostensibly by a British prisoner of war in Germany, entitled "Keep Smiling". Addressing his fellow POWs, the poet urges them,

CARRY ON !

—Reproduced from Punch

Fig.II.13.1: "Carry On"

Despite disillusionment and occasional despair, Victoria's soldier-poets rarely lost a sense of the purpose of the "Great War". Despite the probable morale-boosting purpose of this image, the published poetry suggests that many servicemen did indeed try to "carry on". (*The Western Scot,* 29 December 1915, 5.)

> *Laugh just like brothers together*
>   *Mirth never did one much ill.*
> *Laugh that you've done what your country expected,*
>   *Yes! And you're doing it still!*
> *One peal of laughter makes many,*
>   *Don't put a "grouse" in the way;*
> *Laugh till the game is played right to the end,*
>   *Laugh and just think, "To the Day!"*

(22 October 1917, 4)

Politicians, cartoonists and poets—civilian as well as military—all urged Victoria and the rest of Canada to "carry on".

Much of the verse quoted in this study was written by men who continued to serve even when they intuited the madness of doing so. In place of political commitment, the strongest loyalty which the Victoria soldier expressed was to his companions. This was not expressed in praise of "comradeship", but in verses which were designed to make friends laugh and so to lighten the nearly intolerable burden of trench life. Others wrote poems in order to keep the memory of fallen friends alive.

What distinguished these men was a special kind of bravery. When ideals and preconceptions were battered, most of Victoria's soldier-poets felt the need to maintain discipline and order. We have seen, moreover, how personal values such as honor, duty, modesty and self-respect motivated them. Although perhaps they should have done so, they did not equate these values with "madness". Some of the poets, at least, seem to have understood that they were in thrall to "unjust necessity", and yet they "carried on". There in may lie the tragedy of Victoria's and Canada's "Great" War.

Notes to THE SOLDIERS' WAR EXPERIENCE

1 Launcelot versus Krupp

1 "The lost generation seems resolutely different from us . . . [Poems of the war] speak in language that is unfamiliar today about God, duty, sacrifice and patriotism." [Hope Wolf, reviewing Brian MacArthur (ed)., *For King and Country. Voices from the First World War*, in *Times Literary Supplement* (11 July 2008), 25.]

2 Quoted in Peter Buitenhuis, *The Great War of Words. British, American, and Canadian Propaganda and Fiction, 1914-1933* (Vancouver: University of British Columbia Press, 1987), 47-48.

3 Paul Fussell has described this phenomenon in *The Great War and Modern Memory* (Oxford University Press, 1975).

4 Pierre Berton, *Vimy.* Toronto: McClelland and Stewart, 1986, 35.

5 Sheldon-Williams, *Names Like Trumpets and Other Poems.* [c. 1918], 12. Desmond Morton respectfully notes that few Canadians were the "fearless heroes" of the civilian poetry (*When Your Number's Up* [Toronto: Random House, 1993], 230).

6 Jay Winter, *Sites of Memory, Sites of Mourning. The Great War in European Cultural History* (Cambridge University Press, 1995), 204.

7 "The Revelation", *Rhymes of a Red Cross Man* (London: Benn, 1960), 371.

8 Charles E. Montague, *Disenchantment* (New York: Brentano's, 1922).

9 Robert Nichols (ed.), *Anthology of War Poetry 1914-1918* (London: Nicholson & Watson, 1943), 33.

10 Quoted in Garvin (ed.), *Canadian Poets of the Great War*, 181.

11 Canadian War Records Office. *Canada in Khaki* (London: Cassell and Company, 1917, Vol. I), 172.

12 Nichols, ed., *Anthology of War Poetry 1914-1918*, 22.

13 Will R. Bird, *Ghosts Have Warm Hands. A Portrait of Men at War* (Toronto: Clarke, Irwin, 1968), 146.

14 Modris Ecksteins, *Rites of Spring. The Great War and the Birth of the Modern Age* (Toronto: Lester & Orpen Dennys, 1989), 218.

2 Fight, Canada, for Empire!

1 Laura Lewin, a Victoria journalist, in a poem published in the *Colonist* 2 September 1915, 5.

2 Peregrine Acland, *All Else is Folly. A Tale of War and Passion* (Toronto: McClelland & Stewart, 1929), 27. Elsewhere Acland wrote that this soldier "had fought less as a lover of Britain than as a lover of humanity." (325)

3 Quoted in Read, ed., *The Great War and Canadian Society*, 99.

4 Quoted in Donald Goodspeed, *The Road Past Vimy. The Canadian Corps 1914-1918* (Toronto: MacMillan,1969), 7.

5 David Mackenzie, ed., *Canada and the First World War. Essays in Honour of Robert Craig Brown* (Toronto: University of Toronto, 2005), 36-38.

6 Desmond Morton and J.L. Granatstein, *Marching to Armageddon. Canadians and the Great War 1914-1918* (Toronto: Lester & Orpen Dennis, 1989), 18. See also Margaret Ormsby, *British Columbia. A History,* Vancouver: Macmillan, 1958, 327.

3   Some Feeling Against the English

1   *Over the Top with the 25th [Battalion]. Chronicle of Events at Vimy Ridge and Courcellette* (Halifax: Marshall, 1918), 40.

2   Quoted in Zuehlke, *Brave Battalion*, 103. Canadian soldiers resented being "treated like amateurs", writes Tim Cook. (*At the Sharp End. Canadians Fighting the Great War 1914-1918* [Toronto: Viking, 2007], 530.)

3   Zuehlke, *Brave Battalion,* 165.

4   Bewildered Youths?

1   Quoted in Berton, *Vimy,* 43.

2   Ecksteins, *Rites of Spring,* 191. Martin Stephen refers to the "more simple imperatives" which motivated our grandfathers. (*The Price of Pity. Poetry, History and Myth in the Great W*ar [London: Cooper, 1996], 79).

3   Charles Yale Harrison, *Generals Die in Bed,* (New York: Burt, 1928 [1930]), n.p.

4   Leonard McLeod Gould, *From B.C. to Baisieux. Being the Narrative History of the 102nd Canadian Infantry Battalion,* (Victoria: Cusack, 1919), 86.

5   Gould, *Over the Top,* 39.

6   Canadian War Records Office, *Canada in Khaki,* (London: Cassell and Company, Vol. II, 1917), 172.

7   Harrison, *Generals Die in Bed,* 56.

8   Goodspeed, *The Road Past Vimy*, 44.

9   Stephen, *The Price of Pity*, 84.

10   Eksteins, *Rites of Spring*, 182.

11   *Canada in Khaki,* Vol. II, 172. "Khaki" refers to the dust-colored fabric used in Canadian military uniforms.

12   Kenneth Radley, *We Lead. Others Follow. First Canadian Division 1914-1918* (St. Catharines: Vanwell, 2006), 161.

13   J.E. Wetherell, ed. *The Great War in Verse and Prose* (Toronto: Wilgress, 1919), 124.

14   Desmond Morton and J.L. Granatstein, *Marching to Armaggedon,* 197.

5   A Soldier's Private Values

1   "The Cynics", *Canadian Poems of the Great War*, 131.

2   Sheldon-Williams, *Names Like Trumpets* 13.

3   Lewis, *Over the Top,* 57.

4   Desmond Morton, *When Your Number's Up* (Toronto: Random House, 199), 230.

5   James H. Pedley, *Only This. A War Retrospect* (Ottawa: Graphic Publishers, c. 1927), 150.

6   Quoted in Margaret Ormsby, *British Columbia*, 395-396.

7   Jeffrey A. Keshen, *Propaganda and Censorship during Canada's Great War* (Edmonton, University of Alberta, 1996. 132.

8   Eksteins, *Rites of Spring*, 120.

9   Henry Newbolt, *Poems New and Old*, (Toronto: McClelland & Stewart, 1919), 95.

10 Garvin (ed.), *Canadian Poets of the Great War*, 166.

11 Morton, *When Your Number's Up*, 244.

6   Grub, Tobacco . . . and Rum

1   "European History" (http://europeanhistory.about.com/gi/dynamic/offsite.htm?zi=1/XJ/Ya&sdn=europeanhistory&cdn=education&tm=151&gps=26._)

2   Cook, *At the Sharp End*, 218.

3   Reginald Roy, ed., *The Journal of Private Fraser* (Victoria: Sono Nis, 1985), 79.

4   Service, "The Black Dudeen", *Rhymes of a Red Cross Man, Collected Poems*, 376.

5   Cook, *At the Sharp End*, 383.

6   Printed on large tin cans containing rum, the initials "S.R.D." probably meant "Service Ration Depot", but soldiers read the letters differently.

7   Quoted in Gwyn, *Tapestry of War*, 366.

8   Gould, *From B.C. to Baisieux*, 6.

9   Cook, *At the Sharp End*, 244.

10 Quoted in Cook, *At the Sharp End*, 243.

7   Many a Laugh

1   Anonymous. "Soldiers' Poems". *The Gold Stripe*, 78.

2   Desmond Morton and Glenn Wright, *Winning the Second Battle: Canadian Veterans and the Return to Civilian Life, 1915-1930* (Toronto: University of Toronto Press, 1987), 24.

3   Morton, *When Your Number's Up*, 136.

8   Fighting Fritz

1   Harrison *Generals Die in Bed*, 192.

2   Robert Service, "Only a Boche", Rhymes of a Red Cross Man, *Collected Poems*, 360. He expressed the same attitude in "My Prisoner", *Collected Poems*, 364-366.

3   Eksteins, *Rites of Spring*, 153-4.

4   Montague, *Disenchantment*, 8-9.

5   Morton, *When Your Number's Up*, 138.

6   *The Canadian Front in France and Flanders* (Toronto: Macmillan 1920), 1; and *A Brief Outline of the Story of the Canadian Grenadier Guards and the First Months of the Royal Montreal Regiment in the Great War* (Montreal: Gazette Printing, 1926), 53.

7   *The Gold Stripe*, 78.

9 Our Funny Moods

1   Harry Gregson, *A History of Victoria 1842-1970* (Vancouver: Douglas, 1977), 87.

2   Acland, *Only This*, 89.

3   Charles W. Gordon, *Post Script to Adventure. The Autobiography of Ralph Connor, pseudo.*(New York: Farrar & Rinehart, 1938), 228 and 257-258.

4   Radley, *We Lead. Others Follow*, 371.

5   W.W. Murray ("The Orderly Sergeant"), *Five Nines and Whizbangs,* Ottawa: Perrault (The Legionary Library), l937, 7.

6   Lewis, *Over the Top*, 39.

7   Quoted in Muriel Jarvis Ackinclose, *For the Love of George. In Old Victoria and World War One,* (Victoria [?]: First Choice, 2005), 89.

8   Sheldon-Williams, *Names Like Trumpets*, 12.

9   Nichols, *Anthology of War Poetry 1914-1918*, 95.

10 Quoted in Gwyn, *Tapestry of War,* 139.

10 The Siberian Muddle

1   Benjamin Isitt, "Mutiny from Victoria to Vladivostok, December 1918", *Canadian Historical Review*, Volume 87, Number 2, June 2006, 223-264; and *From Victoria to Vladivostok : Canada's Siberian Expedition, 1917-19* (Vancouver: University of British Columbia, 2010).

2   John Swettenham, *Allied Intervention in Russia 1918-1919 and the Part Played by Canada,* (Toronto: Ryerson, 1967), 172.

11 **Myths and Mysteries**

1   In what follows, I describe what sociologists call "myths". These are collective beliefs that develop in response to the wishes of a group, such as a class or a nation. They are not based on an objective analysis of those wishes but appeal to the group's often unspoken desires.

2   Service, "Rhymes of a Red Cross Man", *Collected Poems,* 300-307.

3   Berton, *Vimy,* 27.

4   Morton, *When Your Number's Up,* 278.

5   Pedley, *Only This, passim*; Bird, *Ghosts Have Warm Hands,* 103.

6   Harrison, *Generals Die in Bed,* 91.

7   *Complete Poems of Marjorie Pickthall,* Toronto: McClelland & Stewart, c. 1927, 194. A similar view was held by Coningsby Dawson in his *The Glory of the Trenches. An Interpretation* (Toronto, Gundy, 1928). According to the book's introduction (written by his father), "the true Glory of the Trenches" was "the Calvaries of a new redemption being wrought out for men by soiled unconscious Christs." (15).

8   Thomas P. Socknat, *Witness against War. Pacifism in Canada 1900-1945* (Toronto: University of Toronto, 1987), 50.

9   Montague, *Disenchantment,* 90-91.

10   Bird, *Ghosts have Warm Hands,* 139.

11   Zuehlke, *Brave Battalion,* 165.

12 Harrison, *Generals Die in Bed*, 212,

13 "The Poetry of the War", *The Gold Stripe*, 34.

14 Sheldon-Williams, *Names like Trumpets,* 13.

15 Jonathan F. Vance, *Death So Noble: Memory, Meaning, and the First World War,* (Vancouver: University of British Columbia Press, 1997).

16 Probably with some pride, on 12 September 1917 (9), the *Times* also published a poem, "The Matchless Maple Leaf" a paeon to the Canadian army, written by an English poet, H. Kendra Baker, but nothing like this came from a local soldier-poet. J.L. Granatstein and Norman Hillmer quote three letters, written about the Battle of Vimy Ridge, but none mentions "nation-building" or Canada. (*Battle Lines. Eyewitness Accounts from Canada's Military History* [Toronto: Thomas Allen, 2004], 149-152).

12 **Censorship and Reality**

1 Bird, *Ghosts Have Warm Hands*, 96.

2 Andrew Wilson, a letter of 14 November 1917, quoted in Granatstein and Hillmer, *Battle Lines*, 183.

3 *Canada in Khaki*, Vol. I, 1917, 86.

4 Berton, *Vimy,* 55.

5 Keshen, *Propaganda and Censorship*, xvi.

6 Nichols, *Anthology*, 62.

7 *The Journal of Private Fraser*, 113.

8   J. M. Winter, *The Great War and the British People* (New York: Palgrave Macmillan, 2003), 291.

9   *Canada in Khaki*, Vol. II, 172.

10   Quoted in Ted Barris, *Victory at Vimy.* 78

11   Ian Hugh Maclean Miller, *Our Glory and Our Grief. Torontonians and the Great War* (Toronto: University of Toronto, 2002), 198.

12   Robert Allen Rutherdale, *Hometown Horizons : Local Responses to Canada's Great War* (Vancouver: University of British Columbia, 2004), xiv.

13   Ernst Jünger, *Storm of Steel. From the Diary of a German Storm-Troop Officer on the Western Front* (London: Chatto and Windus, 1929), 110.

14   Nichols, *Anthology,* 60.

15   Keshen, *Propaganda and Censorship,* 191.

16   Morton and Wright. *Winning the Second Battle, passim.*

13 Carry On!

1   Quoted in H.M. Urquhart, *History of the 16th Battalion (Canadian Scottish)* (Toronto, 1832), 344-46.

THE SOLDIERS' POEMS

S ome poems presented here are not referenced in the text of the book, but are relevant to the work's themes. In a few cases, where I have quoted from a poem in the text, I have not reproduced the whole work here because the entire poem had nothing more of interest to add. This first section includes poems by soldiers who were resident in Victoria and southern Vancouver Island at the time of writing or who were connected to the city in some fashion. When a published poem has an anonymous author, occasionally the editor indicated that the writer was a local poet.

64,976 Canadian men died in the "Great War". Several of these writers were part of that statistic.

B. De M. Andrew

A Victorian's Ode

Don't think of death with fright;
Old Fate, with smirking glee,
Hath spun her nickel bright.

She hides the coin from sight;
It ain't for you and me
To think of death with fright.

She's spun her nickel bright.
'Tis my turn next, maybe,
To beat into the night.

(Colonist, 22 November 1914, 4 [editorial page])

Despite its surprising un-religious nature (in an ostensibly Christian society), the euphemism, "into the night" was popular. So too, was the poem's naïve fatalism.

Anonymous

A Bantam Poem

Caesar was a soldier of maybe five feet four,
And the great Napoleon was certainly no more.
Come and join the Bantams, lads, and improve your rifle
    score,
And you'll go marching to Flanders.

David killed Goliath with a very little stone;
Jack the Giant-Killer had a system all his own.
Come and join the Bantams, lads;
They'll make their valor known,
When they go marching to Flanders.

In the smallest packages the best of goods are brought;
In the choicest settings are the best of diamonds wrought.
Come and join the Bantams; they'll be where the hottest
    fights are fought,
When they go fighting for freedom.

(Colonist, 21 July 1916, 5)

Presumably the author was a Bantam, a man standing below the minimum height of five feet, four inches, required to be accepted as a recruit in the early months of the war. Two Canadian battalions of such men were eventually formed. Something of the bravado of the shorter man is certainly evident here. The author was "a well-known local poet whose works have been widely quoted".

Anonymous

To My Brother-in-Law

You're going, you say, in the Medical Corps,
    You leave wife and children behind;
They need men like you at the seat of the war,
    (And they're not easy to find).
You're high in the service; you couldn't hold back;
    Promotion for you won't be slow;
But, when I suggest that I take the same track,
    You hasten to write me, "Don't go."

The points that you make in your kindly advice
    (For which pray accept my best thanks)
Are, I'm not good enough for an officer's place,
    And something too good for the ranks;
My job is important, my place can't be filled.
    My health isn't up to the test.
There are plenty of men to be wounded or killed,
    To stick where I am would be best.

I answer, the country is calling for men
    To battle for freedom and right;
(That isn't hot from an editor's pen.
    We know why we're into this fight);
They all give up something from comfort to lives,
    I've no one depending on me;
Let those stay at home who have children and wives,
    Just now it's worthwhile to be free.

I've climbed a few hills since the last time we met.
    I've hiked many miles through the woods;
The chief sent me out information to get;
    (He says I've delivered the goods).
My wind is as long as the snow-peak is high
    What I shoot at I frequently hit.
I think I agree with the medical guy,
    Who said, "Put your shirt on, you're fit."

My job is important: I gave it its due;
    I let my two mates go ahead.
There's one who will sail in a fortnight or two,
    And one by this time may be dead.
I wound up the contract, It looks like my turn.
    (My chance of returning is fair.)
And from me and my comrades Old England may learn
    The West raises more than "hot air".

If they can't use my brain, they are free to my brawn,
    But of gangs I have handled a few;
(Experience I've had too severe and [illegible on microfilm]
    With the meanest on earth, which is two);
I've learned mathematics and languages, too.
    Range-finding is quite in my line;
If anyone thinks for subaltern I'd do
    I don't think I need to decline.

(*Colonist,* 23 May 1915, 16)

The author was "a well-known resident of Victoria, a native-born Canadian". Although alert to the existence of misleading propaganda, the poet was sure of the values motivating him. He was fighting for "freedom and right", etc. But who was he? A newspaperman? Joe Gorman? Was his brother-in-law Harry W. Clarke? (See below.)

Anonymous

Making a Soldier

Taking a course at a western school,
Where you walk, and stand, and eat by rule,
Was a subaltern fresh from a rural corps.
The sweat was oozing from every pore,
But he looked at none as they passed that way.
For a sergeant instructor all bronzed and grey,
In stentorian tones would certainly say,
"Now then, Mr. So-and-So, look to your front".

So he held his head, as they say in the book,
As if he was having his picture took.
Then he closed his heels and he clamped his knees
And slapped his hands, at the stand at ease.
He twisted his neck in a soldier's kink,
He fixed his eyes and ceased to wink,
But his weary brain did nothing but think
What the h—is the use of all this?

They placed his fingers and toes just so
They marched him quick and they marched him slow,
And taught him to turn to left and right
Just as he wouldn't attempt in a fight.
The sergeant instructor so bronzed and grey,
With his pacing stick followed him night and day
But beneath his breath God heard him say:
"What a d—old fool the man is."

They stood him at ease, and called him to "'shun",
From half-past nine till half-past one.
They dressed him left and dressed him right,
And they dressed him up for mess at night,
While the sergeant yelled in accents clear
Pages of detail into his ear,
But the only words could the listener hear
From the Sub. was, "this must be discipline".

A lecturing man seized on to him then,
And prated of various warfaring men.
They told him of Welington, Caesar and Ney,
Alexander the Great and the men of his day.
With blackboard and chalk then they told him about
Some turbulent battle or elegant rout,
Till the Sub. was inclined to reply with a shout,
"How about De Wet and Botha?"

They gave him a rifle, a modern L.E.,
And they taught him the manual down to a T.
They showed him the "shoulder", "present" and the "slope",
And his company drill was explained with a rope.

He aimed from the shoulder, he aimed from the knee,
Just in the way they don't shoot now, you see,
Till the Sub. so bewildered, felt ready to hoot,
"Now why in the h—don't they teach me to shoot?"

(*Times,* 4 September 1914, 4 [editorial page])

The "western school" was probably the camp at the Willows Exhibition Grounds in Oak Bay, Victoria. A subaltern was a junior officer. De Wet and Botha were Afrikaner generals in the South African War, 1899-1902. Their Boer soldiers had offered stiff resistance to the British forces. The "L.E." was the Lee Enfield with which, in fact, the Canadian soldier was not originally equipped. The C.E.F.'s Ross Rifle, first supplied, proved faulty and was replaced. But "L.E." rhymes nicely.

Anonymous
Popular entertainers took up on the need for men to affirm their "masculinity". From a musical revue performed in Victoria in 1914:

To Make a Man Out of You

On Sunday I walk out with a soldier
On Monday a sailor for a pard,
On Tuesday, of course, with a B.C. Horse
On Wednesday a Home Guard.

On Thursday I gang out wi' a kiltie,
On Friday a Fusilier or two:
But as you've all been willing,
It didn't need a shilling
To make a man of everyone of you.

"Marching Orders or Shoulder to Shoulder. A Grand Military Musical Review", Royal Victoria Theatre, November 12th, 3th and 14th, 1914.[1]

The word "shilling" refers to the fact that British soldiers and sailors were traditionally paid a shilling when recruited.

Charles Armstrong

It's Up To You

Victoria's proud of her heroes;
Her soldiers have all made good.
Hughes wires for some more and they'll go by the score.
Why, we'd all go along if we could
But some us aren't just the ticket
To be bayoneting Huns in a ditch,
And rheumatics or gout count a bunch of the "but"
Of the fellows who can help "Kitch".

But that doesn't mean, but a jugful,
That there's nothing at all we can do.
We can each do his bit; it's a case of "remit"
And this, gentle reader, means YOU.
We can each bear a good silver rifle,
With a by'net that's pointed with gold.
'Tis a good bit of work that nobody can shirk,
For it takes in the young and the old.

Out there where the shrapnel is bursting,
There's many a man from this town
Who will fearlessly die, feeling sure you and I
Will keep back the wolf from his own.
He's given up home, wife and kiddies;
He's manfully doing his bit;
But his pay isn't big, and so we'll have to dig.
Now are you going to show white, or quit?

There's no use in squirming and dodging;
Here's something that's right up to you.
You can't pack a gun; now are you going to run
From the only small thing you can do?
The boys don't want charity, mind you.
They look upon this as their right.
So come on, get the range, and let go with your change,
And help out the men who can fight.

(*Colonist*, 1 December 1915, 1)

Written on the occasion of the first "War Loan", these verses were printed in a frame on the *Colonist*'s front page.

"Kitch" was Field Marshal Horatio Herbert Kitchener (1850-1916) who was appointed British Secretary of State for War in 1913. He drowned in 1916 when the armored cruiser on which he was sailing struck a mine. "Hughes" was Sir Sam Hughes (1853-1921), Canadian Minister of Militia and Defence.

Armstrong seemed to be fixated on bayonets: see his poem on the subject. He eventually enlisted, leaving wife and child. His stress on acting "manfully" ("showing white") was typical of soldiers' verse. His reference to local servicemen all being "heroes" was also typical. Apart from the fact that the word was losing any meaning, the reference was simply not true in any traditional sense. For example, Lieutenant James Pedley wrote, "We had a couple of men in the company who had been found guilty of desertion and had had the death penalty meted out to them, subsequently altered to two years' imprisonment."[2]

Upon Discovering "Chlorine" in the Morning Cocoa (France 1916)

Thou art no maiden fair to see,
    Chlorine!
And yet, and yet, who canst forget
    Chlorine!
By day I see thee at my feet.
    Chlorine!
Were I at thine, 'twould be more meet.
    Chlorine!
You come, you go, like driven snow.
    Chlorine!
At meals I have my tea with thee,
    Chlorine!
With soup, with fish with ev'ry dish—
    Chlorine!
Yet, while I'm faithful thus to thee,
    Chlorine!

Another claims thy constancy
  Chlorine!
You love, I know our fell M.O.
  Chlorine!
Thou art his strength whate'er betide
  Chlorine!
Long since he claimed thee for his bride
  Chlorine!
Thou'lt at his side in death abide
  Chlorine!
Ah, wanton! When this war is o'er,
  Chlorine!
I pray I'll never see thee more,
  Chlorine!
That thou may'st grace some other place,
  Chlorine!

According to Max Aitken's War Records Office, "The closest watch is maintained by the Army medical authorities over the water supply which Tommy uses in France. All water before it is used is treated with more or less copious quantities of chloride of lime . . . . This adds anything but a pleasant flavour to the beverages and foods into the preparation of which the 'doped' water enters . . . . Many are the supplications which reach the Battalion 'M.O'—medical officer—urging him to omit 'Chlorine' from the cooking water, but invariably, he is adamantine."[3] [Fig. III.1]

The Sniper

All through the pleasant summer day he sits
  Immobile in the shade tree's leafy crest.
About his ears the drowsy sun-fly flits—
  The countryside seems deep in noonday rest.
But now his body stretches, straight and tall—
  A loud report, quick flash of flame,
And there behind yon distant sand-bag wall
  A lad goes down who'll never rise again.

(The Western Scot, 24 May 1916, reproduced in the Western Scot Commemorative Edition, 17)

Fig.III.1: "Water, Water Everywhere, But Not a Drop to Drink!"

Like this hapless soldier, Victoria's war-poets enjoyed few glorious charges, but rum—and fresh water—helped. (Canada in Khaki, Vol. I, 135.)

The *Western Scot,* the publication of the 67th Battalion, appeared every two weeks. Civilians were encouraged to subscribe to it, but how many did so is difficult to ascertain.

Snipers were specialists, trained after 1916 in a two week course on how to stalk the enemy and eliminate him one by one. They were supposed to lower the Germans' morale, restrict their movement, and to kill men who were reckless enough to look out over the top of a trench. They did not usually have to do regular trench chores. Working alone or in pairs, they were also experts in camouflage, operating from purpose-built shelters in a front trench or from trees or ruined houses. The sniper, says Cook, was "a conscious killer".[4]

The memoirist, Will Bird, enjoyed working as a sniper at first. "What a change! We simply went out to the sniping post when we felt like it, came in when we felt like it, had a bit to eat when we felt like it and had more food than I had seen in months." But after shooting three Germans in a row, he refused to shoot a fourth one when the opportunity arose. "A queer sensation had spread over me like nausea . . . . I've had enough . . . I had had all I wanted of sniping . . . That night I could not eat."[5]

Working as snipers, Canadians from the First Nations won a reputation as efficient killers and helped create the image of the Canadian as a superior warrior. In his "The Man From Athabaska", Robert Service presented the "typical" Canadian soldier as an outdoorsman and a crack shot:

> *I'm their exhibition sniper, and they work me like a Dago,*
> *And laugh to see me plug a Boche a half a mile away.*[6]

To the First Draft
Dedicated to Lady Douglas Chapter. Sailed from Victoria on Overseas Service on August 26 1914, Wearing Sprigs of Heather, the Gift of the Lady Douglas Chapter, I.O.D.E. [Imperial Order of the Daughters of the Empire]

Just a sprig o' Island heather,
  Such as they wore that sad day
When they broke each tie and tether,
  And so bravely marched away.

To their ears the ringing "Rally!"
  Was command and argument.
Bargaining not they did not dally;
  Swift to answer quick they went.

Fighting, suff'ring, conqu'ring, dying,
  With the best the Maple gave,
Each with each in valor vying,
  They found glory—and the grave.

Ypres and Dickebusche both knew them,
  And the mud-fed, blood-red Somme.
Festubert could not undo them—
  Countless battles "sans le nom."

Each took toll of their slim numbers
  (Nought their courage could abridge),
And it flamed amid the thunders
  On the heights of Vimy Ridge.

Few are left that wore the heather
  Such a brief, short time ago;
But that they fought true, together
  Holding Honor high, we knew!

Not in sorrow but with gladness
  With the joy that pride imparts;
But with just a touch of sadness
  We wear their badge above our hearts.

(*Times*, 28 August 1917, 15)

   Here Armstrong enjoys the romantic rhetoric still popular with some poets. In this poem, he makes the only reference to the Battle of Vimy Ridge in Victoria soldiers' published poetry.

The Battle of Festubert occurred in May 1915; the Battle of the Somme, in July 1916. Dickebusche is the site of a British military cemetery in Flanders.

When I Kick in

When I kick in—
(God knows how it may come)
There, in the muck of some shell-shattered plain,
After long hours of misery in the rain,
There'll be no tuck and roll of muffled drum
When I kick in.

When I kick in—
Just think the best of me:
Think of the good things I had hoped to do,
Forgetting those I'd done were all too few,
Some part lives on. Just plant the rest of me
When I kick in.

When I kick in—
Just send along a line:
To tell Her and the Boy I needed them—
That all my love my heart conceded them,
And I am waiting where the Great Suns shine,
When I kick in.

(The Western Scot, 19 July 1916, and The Western Scot Commemorative Edition, 43)

Fig.III.2: "Jump Into It!"

The image on a Victory Bond campaign of 1918 might give Victoria civilians the impression that most local soldiers used their bayonets in aggressive hand-to-hand combat entered into with athletic zeal. The reality was different. (*Victoria Daily Colonist,* 31 October 1918, 4.)

To the British Bayonet

From old Bayonne
There comes a pet
Of British Tommies, "rook" and "vet"—
The peerless, piercing bayonet.

On many a field
Has it been wet,
This pointed, perfect, pretty pet—
The peerless, piercing bayonet.

The want of men
Who can't forget
The reek of Belgium's bloody sweat—
The peerless, piercing bayonet.

The German foe
Shall pay his debt
Of death unto this pretty pet—
The peerless, piercing bayonet.

The Western Scots
Without regret
Shall use this perfect piercing pet
Upon the foe who hands are wet
With helpless Belgium's bloody sweat.
This pointed perfect, pretty pet—

From old Bayonne—
The Bayonet.

(The Western Scot, 20 November 1915, no. 7, 8; in *Western Scot*
Commemorative Edition, 12)

Robert Service also eulogized the bayonet in "My Bay'nit",
although not as a dangerous weapon:

When first I left Blighty they gave me a bay'nit
    And told me it 'ad to be smothered wiv gore; . . .

At toasting a biscuit me bay'nit's a dandy;
I've used it to open a bully beef can;
For pokin' the fire it comes in werry 'andy;
For any old thing but for stickin' a man[7]

Although Service did not see active combat, he understood the soldier's attitude to his "bay'nit" better than Armstrong did. (The Victoria man had not left for France when he wrote his poem.) Fewer than 1% of Canadian soldier's wounds were from bayonet attacks.[8] [Fig.III.2] "Blighty" was the British soldier's slang for Britain.

This weapon, however, was good for opening tins of bully beef, toasting bread and encouraging prisoners to move along quickly. [Fig.III.3] One soldier-poet describes how he accidentally gashed himself with his own "blade". (See below.) The bayonet affixed to the notoriously ineffective Ross rifle could fall off during firing. Nevertheless, writes Cook, the bayonet remained the final weapon at the soldier's disposal. Its seventeen inches made a rifle a spear, possibly giving a sense of security. Moreover, many Canadian dead whose bodies were never found may have been killed by German bayonets.[9]

Fig.III.3: "Everything Has Its Uses"

Opening a tin (probably of "bully beef"), this soldier employed his bayonet for survival, but not in combat. Another cartoon in Canada in Khaki shows a soldier roasting a chicken impaled on his bayonet. (*Canada in Khaki*, Vol. I, 54.)

The Fallen Bell

On coming upon a cracked and fallen bell, on Christmas Eve, in the ruins of a Belgian village back of the firing line. The bell speaks:

How can I sing glad tidings of great joy?
    How can I ring a message to mankind?
No more may I my ancient tongue employ
    To fling a clam'rous greeting down the wind
Such nights as this in happier times of peace,
    Surmounting all the warm-lit hamlet's glee,
My deep-voiced tones boomed forth and did not cease
    While e'er my masters held their revelry.
Old Jan would swing upon my hempen curl
    And laugh with prideful pleasure at my song.
The while his cronies' harmless quips would hurl
    And wonder he could humour me so long.
Alas! Old Jan is gone, and all his kind;
    Their simple pleasures too are long forgot
And all the friends I've know time out of mind
    Swept by the common hurricane—are not!

        *   *   *   *

Tonight once more, it is the Eve of Christ;
    The mitrailleuse, the bomb, alone we hear.
Amid the wreckage of my throne envised
    I lie song-dumb and desolate, and drear.
I pray you, alien friend, to bury me
    Here in the debris of my chosen spot,
That with familiar things I still may be,
    And, with familiar things, corrode—and rot!

France 1916
(Canadian War Records Office, *Canada in Khaki,* Vol. I, 36)

When, in Chapter II, Armstrong imagined a young soldier encouraging his moustache to grow because "Your King and Country need you . . ." *(The Western Scot Commemorative Edition,* 10), he was reacting to the ban on shaving the upper lip during 1914-1916, because certain military authorities believed that a moustache helped men to aim their rifles. Perhaps the mustache was also considered a sign of a warrior's necessary "masculinity". In 1916 a British soldier composed this verse on the subject.

> *Has everybody got his clean socks on?*
> *Has everybody washed his feet?*
> *Is everybody letting his mustache grow?—*
> *Not long but very neat.*
> *For these are the things that count most*
> *In the war with Germany*[10]

William Joseph Beale

The Lay of Liège

> *Lord Attila of Potsdam*
> *By the Rhine gods he swore*
> *That the great House of Zollern*
> *Should keep the peace no more.*
> *By the Rhine gods he swore it*
> *And named a trysting day,*
> *And sent his ultimatums forth*
> *East and West and South and North*
> *To start the great affray.*
>
> *East and West and South and North*
> *The messages go fast,*
> *And tower and town and cottage*
> *Have heard the trumpet's blast.*
> *Shame on the false Italian*
> *Who lingers in his home,*
> *When Attila of Potsdam*
> *Is on the march alone.*
>
> *The horsemen and the footmen*
> *Are pouring in amain,*
> *Though Italy's a loss to him*
> *Friend Austria is a gain.*
> *From many a Hunnish hamlet*
> *Through woods of beech and plane*

His warriors hest with eagle crest,
Now move in solid line.

From lordly Unter Linden
Where scowls the far-famed bold,
The warlord now goes forth to war
Like a godless king of old.
The harvests of the Hunland
This year old men shall reap;
This year young girls be mourning,

While widowed mothers weep;
And in the vats of Pilsen
This year the must shall glance
Round the white feet of laughing girls
Whose sires have marched to France.

And nearer fast and nearer
Doth the red whirlwind come
And louder still and still more loud
From underneath that rolling cloud,
Is heard the trumpet's war-note proud,
The trampling of the Hun,
And the banner of proud Attila
Is seen amidst them all,
The terror of the Belgian,
The terror of the Gaul.

While somewhere with his army,
O'er looking all the war,
Lord Attila of Potsdam
Sits in his motor car.
And by his side Augustus,
Prince of the Latian [sic] name,
Takes lesson from his father
Of how to play the game.

Now, out spake gallant Leman,
Against the fort of Liège
The serried hosts advance
Ten thousand times ten thousand—

Upon their way to France.
The captain at the gate:
"To every man upon this earth
Death cometh soon or late;
And how can man die better
Than facing fearful odds
For the ashes of the fathers
And the temples of his gods?"

To him quoth all the fortmen:
"For love of hearth and home,
We'll stem the tide of Vandal lust,
So let the Vandal come!"
And as that host with measured tread,
With guns out-belching, marched ahead,
The dying mingling with the dead,
While four whole days and nights were sped,
Our earth looked on with pride.

Far o'er the crashing forest
The giant arms lie spread,
And the pale augurs muttering low
Gaze on the blasted head.
But now no sound of laughter
Was heard among the foes.
A wild and dreadful clamor
From all the vanguard rose.
Six furlong lengths from the entrance
Halted that deep array,
And for a space no man came forth.
Was none who would be foremost;
To lead such dire attack;
But those behind cried Forward!
And those before cried back!
And backward moves, and forward,
Wavers the brief array;
And on the tossing sea of steel
To and fro the standards reel
And the victorious trumpet-peal
Dies fitfully away.

Now in the years before us
When the cold night winds blow
And the barking of the watchdogs
Is heard amidst the snow:
When round the lonely cottage
Roars loud the tempest's din
And the good logs of the farmer
Roar louder yet within.

When the good man mends his ploughshare
And cleans his pruning hook
When the good wife plies her needle
And the grandsire reads his book,
With weeping and with laughter
Still is the story told
How well those Belgians held the forts
In the brave days of old.

(*Colonist,* 30 September 1914, 13)

This poem is the finest example of the hold which nineteenth century traditional romantic language and imagery had on Victoria's poets in 1914. Were we not assured from other sources that this poet is in earnest, his work might be comic. Yet the *Colonist*'s editors, as did many readers, took it seriously. Many readers would hear the echoes of Thomas Babington Macaulay (1800-1859) from their schooldays' reading. In 1842, he published his "Lays of Ancient Rome", a collection of ballads about heroic events in classical history. Beale's verse that begins "Then out spake gallant Leman" is an almost literal copy of a verse in Macaulay's "Horatius", which describes the Roman defence of a bridge against the Tuscan army:

Then out spake brave Horatius,
The Captain of the Gate:
"To every man upon this earth
Death cometh soon or late.
And how can man die better
Than facing fearful odds,
For the ashes of his fathers,
And the temples of his Gods".

Encircled by modern forts of steel and concrete, Liège was "the gate to Belgium". On August 5-6 1914, the Germans attacked, but not until 16 August did the city surrender. The Belgians' resistance helped to slow down the overall German onslaught into France and caused them loss of valuable time. The frustration and surprise of their soldiers may have led to some of the atrocities much reported on at the time.[11]

"Unter Linden" is a reference to Unter den Linden, the main avenue (lined with linden trees) in the heart of Berlin. "The false Italian" refers to Italy which had been allied to Germany and Austria, which yet remained neutral, not honoring its putative commitments in the "Triple Alliance". Later, the Italians sided with France, Britain and Russia.

Responding to the Boxer Rebellion in China and the murder of the German ambassador there, on 27 July 1900 Emperor William II urged departing German soldiers to be as savage as he imagined Attila the Hun to have been centuries before. His reference to the Huns was taken up by journalists later as a description of the Germans. The Vandals were a Germanic tribe which sacked Rome in the fifth century C.E. General Gerard Mathieu Leman (1851-1920) was in charge of the forts defending the city of Liège.

James H. Brewton

To General Sir Arthur W. Currie
(By a "returned soldier")

We hail thee! Leader of those—our sons
Who pledged their lives upon the fields of France:
And, daring all, went forward those long years,
Leaving a name a glory that will live
Imperishable. Not glory did they seek,
Their goal the World's redemption,
And a Peace that would be always.
Gaining thereby a heritage to bless
Our children's children; and a right
For the oppressed and weak to live and flourish.

To you, their chief, we would fain pay honor,
Becoming to Canada's greatest son.
Thy skill we honor,
But greater still the strength and faith
That made you brave and strong those fearful years,
When weighty care went hand in hand with carnage,
And pain and sacrifice were all about thee.
Then were you tried for those who knew thee
Knew thy great heart, and knew thy tenderness
Serene through all in knowledge of the Right
That must prevail—and so you "carried on"
Nor needed words of spleen, nor petty spite
From those who sought thy place. No trick of fortune yours
Nor help to rise, but all the traits of greatness
And faith and skill have led up the ladder.
So we who knew thee in this western Isle,
Greet thy return with special joy and pride;
Here since your early teens you gave your best
To learn and teach the rudiments of war,
Taking each step and rank, and then at last
Your place—a leader in the van with those
Who sprang to arms when the first bugle blew.
Since when each passing year has marked your place
Until at last you led our arms; and with each battle won—
Fresh laurels have evinced your worth.
Not we alone, but from the far Atlantic
To this West shore—all Canada salutes thee;
As one who nobly led her glorious sons
To Victory and Peace. We thank you for your part
From hearts forever grateful. Your name
Honored and sung through future generations
Will be a guide and inspiration
To all that follow after.

(*Colonist,* 5 October 1919, 4)

Sir Arthur William Currie (1875-1933) was commander
of the First Canadian Division, appointed September 1915.
A former teacher and realtor, his only military experience had
been as Colonel of the militia unit, the Gordon Highlanders of

Victoria. Although clumsy in demeanor and looks, and lacking both "the common touch" and oratorical skill, he turned out to be a natural warrior. His attention to detail and openness to innovation helped to give the Canadians their reputation as superior fighters, as was exemplified in the Second Battle of Ypres in April 1915 and at Vimy Ridge in June 1917. Understanding the lethal effects of modern military technology, he insisted on keeping casualties as few as possible. With his flexibility and refusal to follow outmoded practices, he was possibly the best soldier that Canada has ever produced. He visited Victoria on 6 October 1919.

Inflated rhetoric was still in use after the Great War. The use of blank verse, however, was relatively new in popular poetry. Oddly, the poet makes no mention of Currie's real accomplishments on the battlefield! His concern for "a Peace that would be always" was a widespread hope, soon to be disappointed. The tribute is deserved, for, although an "Arthur Currie Lane" and a "Currie Road" are found in Victoria, the man is little known in the city today where his name is no longer an "inspiration".

Similarly, an anonymous civilian poem ("to Sir Arthur Currie") in the *Colonist* (10 September 1919, 4), praises Currie, "a true knight" for his devotion to "Duty", his defence of "Justice" and his love of Canada. The appeal to the romantic image of a knight is typical as is the reference to duty and justice, but the praise for his Canadian patriotism is unusual.

Harry W. Clarke

His One Request

He was only a laddie from Scotland,
  Who scarcely could claim twenty years,
With the face of a boy and the frame of a man
  And a voice to delight Scottish ears.

He was weary and homesick and lonely,
For he was one who had been
Almost a year at the business,
Felt it and smelt and seen.

We were feeding him on soft food and milk slops,
Of which he did sorely complain
So one day to tickle his palate
We asked for a dish he could name.

He asked for no French named concoction,
In the auld guid braid Doric it came,
"Man, would ye no gie's a bit tattie
It would surely remind me o' hame."

And now he is back in the homeland,
He lives on a diet fu' plain,
But of tatties and milk sure he'll thrive grand,
And be glad to be there just the same.

(*Colonist,* 25 May 1916, 5)

During Clarke's service with a British Field Ambulance unit, he may have had this experience. His poem is a good example of the sentimental attachment which many Victorians had to the "old country". "Tatties" are mashed potatoes. (A statue of the popular Scottish poet, Robert Burns, stands in Victoria's Beacon Hill Park.)

A.A. Connon

The Survivor

With apologies to the author of 'The Crew of the Nancy Brig' and also to No. 1 Company, 67th Battalion.

On Wednesday last, as the Willows I passed,
I met with a Private bold.
He'd the air of a Colonel, so great and eternal
And this is the story he told.

"Oh, I am the Major and Subalterns four,
       The Captain and Q.M.S.
I'm non-coms galore, the guard at the door,
       And the cook of the Company Mess."

Then I wondered if he could be strictly T.T.
       Yet he seemed to be able though old.
And his eye twinkled bright with sparks of delight
       As again the same story he told—

"Yes, I am the Plaquets, the Guards and Fatigues,
       The prisoners in their cell.
The Sergeant gruff and the Corporal bluff,
       And the C.S.M. as well."

Then I pondered, you see, how this wonder could be,
       And this man with these ranks who'd endow.
Till he said with great glee, "I'm the only one free
       From the mumps in my Company now.

Yes, I am the Major and Subalterns four
       The Captain and Q.M.S.,
The noncoms galore, the guard at the door,
       And the cook of the Company Mess."

(*Colonist,* 20 February 1916, 10)

"Q.M.S." refers to the rank of Quartermaster Sergeant; "C.S.M.", to that of Company Sergeant Major. A plaquet was a form of armor.

Route marches beginning before dawn and sleeping in wet canvass tents caused health problems at the Willows in Victoria. See also Rifleman Shepherd's lament over the weather.

Connon may have been thinking of W.S. Gilbert's "Yarn of the Nancy Bell", part of which reads,

Oh, I am a cook and a captain bold,
And the mate of the NANCY brig,
And a bo'sun tight, and a midshipmite,
And the crew of the captain's gig.

Edwin Freeman

Resthaven

Back home in Canada, is it really true?
After all the hardships I have gone through.
Yes, it is true, here are the old pine trees
And dear old "Resthaven" by the silver sea.

Here all is peace, the "Sisters" are so kind,
They understand us boys, they are not blind.
They bear with us, in all our funny moods,
For well they know, our nerves are anything but good.

No matter when you want them, they are always there
With a bright smile your troubles to share.
To cheer you up, when you feel awful blue
And say: "don't be downhearted, we will pull you through."

Way out in Flanders I have often dreamed
Of scenes that somehow fit in with these.
A nice white bed, lot of nice things to eat,
Away from all this mud, this strife, this heat.

And I am here at last, it's really true.
It is no dream I have gone through,
I am awake, I see things as they are;
I am so glad, so far away from care.

Why I was spared to come back I do not know
But I'm so happy here, and I should like to show
To all these "Sisters" here, who have given up their homes
To make us boys happy, how much we owe.

Now here's to all the "Sisters" at "Resthaven" by the sea,
For they sure are the nicest bunch that you have ever seen,
And no matter where I wander or wherever I may roam,
I shall always think of "Resthaven" as Home Sweet Home.

(*Colonist,* 28 January 1917, 12)

This poem may verge on the trite but Freeman's verse gives a rare hint of the horrors of the trenches and the difficulties of adjusting to physical and psychological wounds. His sincerity contrasts vividly with the inflated verbiage of earlier soldier-poets' rhetoric and especially with that of many civilian poets. Freeman had been part of "the Fighting Seventh Battalion".

Resthaven "Convalescent Home" was one of several established by the Military Hospitals Commission in British Columbia. Situated on a small island at Sidney, not far from Victoria, it was reached by boat or a bridge. Originally a private home, it was renovated and equipped for medical uses, and operated by Major J.S. Harvey, himself a wounded veteran. Many returned soldiers received vocational training as well as medical treatment here. Tennis courts and a cricket pitch offered opportunities for sport. "Work and play," said the *Colonist,* "under the tactfully administered rules of military discipline, are combined to lead minds which tend to brood on morbid memories of the past . . .".[12]

Leonard McLeod Gould

Dawn

These lines were written during the interval between the 2nd Battle of Arras and the 2nd Battle of Cambrai [1918].

Dawn! And the sky grows brighter.
The darkness and mist disappear;
Passed are the shadows of evening,
The things that we fought for grow clear;
And the doubts that have troubled the nations
Are stilled, as our triumph draws near.

Dawn! And the night shrinks cowering.
The Powers of Darkness decrease.
Soon o'er the ruins of Europe
Will hover the Angel of Peace;
And the lives that the struggle has parted
Will meet, when all warfare shall cease.

Dawn! And this Christmas morning
Brings hope to a suffering world.
E'en now from their tottering strongholds
The Forces of Evil are hurled;
And the nations are banded together
'Neath the banner of Freedom unfurled.

(Reprinted from the Battalion Christmas Card, 1918. *From B.C. to Baisieux. Being the Narrative History of the 102ⁿᵈ Canadian Infantry Battalion,* Victoria: Cusack, 1919, 86.)

Gould expresses what many civilians and servicemen hoped for—a lasting peace—an ideal which would never be reached in the postwar years. Probably one of the causes of the failure to "win the peace" was the notion that Germany represented the "Forces of Evil".

The Runners. An Appreciation
(Inspired by the Runners of the 102ⁿᵈ Canadian Infantry Battalion)

When soldiers are ready to drop with fatigue,
And only an Adjutant's brain can intrigue
A vital dispatch to the C.O.'s colleague;
Who are the boys who can still stay a league?
        The Runners.

When wires are broken, and pigeons won't fly,
When shrapnel and whiz-bangs are bursting on high
When hell's on the earth, and earth's in the sky;

Who are the boys who will get through or die?
        The Runners.
So here's to all soldiers of every degree,
Be they horsemen, or gunners, or stout infantry

But specially those who appeal most to me
Who tackle their work with a semblance of glee.
The Runners.

(*Canada in Khaki,* Vol. II, p. 20; and *From B.C. to Baisieux,* 4)

A "C.O." is a commissioned officer. Runners were soldiers who maintained communication with headquarters by literally running back and forth three or four times a day with messages. "I found the runners for the most part silent, sleepless men," wrote James Pedley; "each man of a pair was usually much attached to his mate and the risky nature of their work won them everyone's respect. Runners and signalers alike had often warm quarters when the other boys were freezing in the trench . . . . When Fritz put on a strafe . . . you might . . . hear the heavy breathing of a pair of runners trotting with a message through the shrapnel storm."[13] See also Sheldon-Williams' poem, "Runners of the Somme". "Whizbangs" were small high-velocity shells which made a whizzing noise before they struck.

The Call to the 102nd
(Comox-Atlin. Battalion, C.E.F.)

There was a sound of carpentry by night.
        And Comox' plains re-echoed to the din,
Of those that labored hard at building huts
        To house the Comox-Atlin soldiers in.
For war's alarms had spread abroad the land
        And every town and hamlet sent its men
To swell the grim batallions raised in haste
        To tour and beard the Kaiser in his den.

And so it was that on Vancouver's Isle
        Far from the madding crowds that throng the towns
A force of men assembled on the coast,
        And formed their camp on Comox' sandy downs,
A stalwart band, not drawn from city clerks.
        But from the ranks of those that breathe the air
Which God had given free to them who have the wit
        To live in open spaces, free from care.

As when the clarion voice of Chanticleer
 Rings out to greet the dawn and summons forth
A waking world to labor and to toil,
 So went the call to east, to South, to West, to North,
A call for men, red-blooded men and true
 For men of grit, for men whose faith was strong,
For men e'en willing to lay down their lives,
 To battle for the weak, to right the wrong.

And, as the scattered members of a flock
 Return at sunset to the shepherd's call
Nor linger not nor loiter on the way
 But urgent seek for shelter ere night fall
So came the men. Some heard the summons dread
 In lonely solitudes, and, hearing left,
Their toilsome work of felling giant trees,
 Which, fallen and of boughs and limbs bereft,
Are fashioned to man's use. These heard and came.
 Another band from those who drive the mills
And prove man's mast'ry over Nature's stores
 Of coal and iron hidden in the hills
Obeyed the call, and, casting down their tools
 Came hastening from all sides and signed their names
Upon the register of fame, as unafraid
 Men trained to war by aptitude in games.

Nor was the race of Cinncinatus dead,
 Who left his plough and donned the general's cloak
When Rome stood doomed. Through harvest field and farm
 The challenge rang to men with hearts of oak.
Nor did they fail. Their pruning-hooks they changed
 For Mars' dread arms, and, faithful, pledged their lives.

See, from the womb of Earth springs forth a troop!
 What men are these? As round the Summer hives
We see the honey bees each bearing home
 The sweetness it has gathered through the day,
So are these men, who labor underground
 To wrest from Nature all the wealth they may.

And thus they came—from forest, mine and mill,
To serve the King, whom God shall keep from ill.

(*Colonist,* 16 July 1916, 5)

Gould's knowledge of ancient history was not unusual at the time. Cinncinatus was the first elected leader of the Roman empire, mandated to defend Rome against its enemies which he did successfully. He seems also to have recalled reading Lord Byron's "Eve of Waterloo" which begins, "there was sound of revelry bynight . . .". Typically, Gould claims that own colleagues were "trained to war by aptitude in games."

Song of the Spit
(Sung to the tune of "John Brown's Body")

We're Warden's weary warriors, a drilling on the sand.
And paying out a buck a day to help the bloomin' band.
But what they do with all the cash, we don't quite understand,
       As we go marching on.

The Colonel forms us up in line and hands us lots of bull;
"You are the finest bunch of men that trigger e'er did pull."
On beef and beans and bread and jam we keep our
       bellies full,
       As we go marching on.

The sand get in our blankets and the wind blows chill
       and drear.
If life was dull at Comox, it's a damned sight duller here,
You have to go a mile or so to get a glass of beer,
       As we go marching on.

Chorus:
We are Warden's weary warriors,
We are Warden's weary warriors,
We are Warden's weary warriors,
The gallant One-O-Two.

(From B.C. to Baisieux. Being the Narrative History of the 102nd Canadian Infantry Battalion. Victoria: Cusack, 1919, 4)

Gould's truculent skepticism was often the recruit's first reaction to training, echoed by the anonymous soldier at the Willows who asked "What the h—is the use of all this?" (See above.) "Warden" was Lieutenant-Colonel J.W. Warden. Comox, with its fine harbor, lies 150 miles north of Victoria on Vancouver Island's east coast. In the nineteenth century, the nearby Goose Spit, a narrow peninsula of sand, enabled the Imperial Navy to use the area for training.

Come In!
(With apologies to the shade of Lewis Carroll)

"Will you join in my battalion?" Said a sergeant to a male:
"There's a purpose in my asking, but I guess you know the tale.
See how eagerly the Germans and the Austrians get in groups.
They are waiting on the frontier—will you come and join the troops?
Will you, won't you, will you, won't you, will you join the troops?
Will you, won't you, will you, won't you, will you join the troops?"

You really have no notion how fine will be the how-de-do.
When once you've joined the khaki and joined the One-O-Two"
But the slacker turned a weary eye, he said, "What, give up soups?"
And he thanked the sergeant kindly, but he would not join the troops.
Would not, could not, would not, could not, would not join the troops.
Would not, could not, would not, could not, would not join the troops.

> *"What matters it how far we go?" his sergeant friend*
>   *replied.*
> *"There is another shore, you know, upon the other side.*
> *The further off from Canada, the nearer to Berlin.*
> *The water's fine, be not afraid, make up your mind,*
>   *COME IN.*
> *Will you, won't you, will you, won't you, join and be a man?*
> *Will you, won't you, will you, won't you? Come, help us*
>   *all you can."*

(*Colonist*, 5 February 1916, 5)

Gould's enthusiasm was typical of many volunteers, with their illusions about a "fine how-de-do" and advancing as far as the German capital. The appeal to an ideal of masculinity was also common. "The Lobster-Quadrille", by Lewis Carroll, begins:

> *"Will you walk a little faster?" said a whiting to a snail,*
> *"There's a porpoise close behind us, and he's treading*
>   *on my tail.*
> *See how eagerly the lobsters and the turtles all advance!*
> *They are waiting on the shingle—will you come and join*
>   *the dance?*
> *Will you, won't you, will you, won't you, will you join the*
>   *dance?*
> *Will you, won't you, will you, won't you, won't you join*
>   *the dance?"*

R.A.L.

A Parody

The "Elegy Written in a Country Church-Yard" by Thomas Gray was lampooned by "a Victoria boy at present in training in Shorncliffe Camp, England".

> *The trumpet sounds "Lights Out!" at close of day,*
> *I see Grand Rounds wind slowly o'er the lea.*
> *The yawning sentry plots his weary way,*
> *And leaves the camp to darkness and to me.*

Now fade the glimmering candles that we buy,
And for a few short hours a stillness holds,
Save where a man with midnight pass reels by,
Or night's made hideous by the men with colds.

Save where from yonder lines a harsh note strikes,
And blatant bugles to the moon proclaim
That each man may default as oft he likes,
So long as when required he speaks his name.

Beneath those bell-tents, old, and torn and frayed,
Where reeks the air, and many a strange thing creeps,
Deep in his blankets thick, and bed unmade,
Each weary, dreary, beery soldier sleeps.

The breezy call each morn, "Get out of bed"—
The sergeant's cursing each one with a grouch,
The ord'ly corp'r'ral's call for sick and dead,
Can scarcely raise them from their lowly couch.

For them each day the cookhouse fires do burn,
The sergeant-major vents his daily wrath;
All sorts of movements queer they try to learn,
And dine each day on mulligan or broth.

Oft do their savings to the canteen yield,
Three weeks each month they generally are broke.
How skillfully their knives and forks they wield,
How laugh they at the sergeant-major's jokes!

Let not headquarters mock their lack of toil,
Their awkward gait, their drill-evading tricks.
Nor M.O.'s hear with a disdainful smile
The weak and lame excuses of the sick.

Nor you, ye Home Guard, think it not a crime
If daily on their boots no shine they raise,
If buttons, tarnish, tunics cake with grime,
When they must sleep in them for days and days.

The boast of ribbons, nor the pomp of spurs,
Nor all the stripes of which a man could think,
Can keep canteens open after hours.
The paths of pleasure lead but to the clink.

(*Colonist,* 23 June 1917, 4)

"When you were nearly crazy", wrote Acland, "when the men around you were nearly crazy, when crazy men with gray faces and staring eyes were crawling past your feet, you had to make jokes, however rotten they were, to keep yourself sane."[14] Moreover, perhaps between the lines of this poem is the writer's sense that the high-minded rhetoric of the original had little relevance in the twentieth-century. (But his high school English teacher would have been pleased to know that he remembered Gray's work.)

Kenneth George Halley

In Memoriam

Dead on the field of honor, that old story
Which all past ages of our history tell,
You gave our life, you all, for Britain's glory,
And so we lost you, we who loved you well.

Cheerful and kind, freehanded, open-hearted,
Smiling alike 'mid sunshine or 'mid rain;
Little we thought that on the day we parted,
We'd never see your face in life again.

True as your steel you faced the battle's dangers.
Smiling at Death, who reaped by day and night.
Now though you lie beneath the soil of strangers
Fearless you fell, upholding what was right.

God rest you, boy, though foreign sod lies o'er you
Quiet you sleep, where all is now at peace.
Those still to fall, and those who fell before you
All give their lives that future strife may cease.

So we must strive to follow your example,
Doing our best—just all that men can do.
No foe on earth on Britain's flag shall trample
While she breeds sons and soldiers such as you.

If before long it happens that you meet us;
If, khaki-clad, we meet your honored end,
By the Dark Portal well we know you'll greet us,
Clasping hour hands in shadowland, old friend.

(*Colonist,* 23 September 1915, 5)

Halley wrote this upon hearing of the death of his Salt Spring Island friend, Lieutenant A.G. Kemp, who had been serving with the Royal Warwickshire Regiment and was killed in action in the Dardanelles Campaign on 15 August 1915. Halley had not yet enlisted.

His language is full of the rhetorical verbosity of the time with reference to concepts of "honor" and "glory", love of England, and death as a sleep. Euphemisms such as the "dark portal" and "shadowland" suggest a gloomy view of the afterlife with little Christian hope. But Halley is both optimistic and illusioned. Kemp, he says, "smiled at Death" and fell "fearlessly". How did he know how Kemp died? The truth may have been different. "I have seen pictures in the movies and in pictorial papers of the boys going 'over the top' with smiling, cheery faces," wrote Private W.C. Millar. "Personally, I have grave doubts as to where these pictures were taken . . . . We all knew only too well that, before we reached the enemy positions, thousands of machine gun bullets would be facing us as well as shell-fire, bombs, minnenwerfers, rifle grenades, and the final bayonet thrust when we reached our goal."[15]

The Face at Courcelette:
An incident of the night of September 15, 1916

The circling smoke when the shrapnel broke was an
    awe-inspiring sight,
And the shells came in with a deafening din and a
    blinding blaze of light;

But of all the sights of those dreadful nights there's one I
*   can't forget—*
It's a fire-swept space, and a soldier's face on the ridge
*   near Courcelette.*

The night was bright with the star shell's light and a full
*   moon over head,*
And it seemed to sigh, as it gazed from high at the ranks
*   of scattered dead:*
But the dead slept sound on the trampled ground, in their
*   gray or khaki dress,*
And for them at least all this hell had ceased, and they'd
*   earned their endless rest.*

But one lay still on the muddy hill, and he seemed to bid
*   me stay.*
So I left the trench on the limestone bench for the place
*   where the soldier lay,*
With his clothes all mud, and his breast all blood, and his
*   feet in a gun-wheel rut.*
With his stiff left hand on his rifle band and his right on
*   the broken butt.*

Then I heard no more of the awful roar, and the scream
*   of the iron tide*
As it swept the place, for I saw this face as I knelt by the
*   dead man's side.*

'Twas the face, I knew, of a man who'd go to the mouth of
*   a hostile gun,*
Of a man who knew what he had to do, and who felt that
*   his work was done.*

Who had done his best and who'd earned his rest, where
*   the voices of war are still.*
For I read that look like an open book, as I knelt on the
*   shell swept hill;*
His bayonet gleamed in the light that streamed as the
*   brilliant star shells broke.*
Then calm and clear to my shell stunned ear it seemed
*   that the dead voice spoke.*

*"My day is done and my race is run, and I'm one that
    has to pay,*
*But I'd rather fall at my country's call than be one who
    stayed away.*
*Our work's not done, it has just begun, in spite of the
    thousands gone,*
*So we leave you here, and your duty's clear—It's for you
    to 'carry on'."*

*Then I heard a call from the sand-bagged wall and it cut
    thro' my numbing brain,*
*Till I heard the roar of the guns once more and the
    scream of the iron rain.*
*So I left him there in the star shell's glare, while the
    moon frowned overhead,*
*For my place was then with the living men, and not with
    the useless dead.*

*The days fly fast and a long time's past since I climbed
    from the blown-in trench*
*And knelt by the side of the man who died on the muddy
    lime-stone bench.*
*Tho' many nights show their fearful sights, still there's
    one I can't forget*
*It's the moonlit space and the still dead face of the man
    at Courcelette.*

(*Colonist,* 16 December 1916, 4)

Halley was with the First Pioneers at Courcelette, in mid-September 1916.

All three divisions of the Canadian Corps were involved in that battle, where the creeping barrage was used for first time. A wall of shells crept forward just ahead of advancing troops in hundred-yard lines at three-minute intervals. Despite this innovation, the encounter with the Germans was an attritional battle costing Canadians 24,029 casualties.[16] One of the commanding officers wrote in his diary: "If hell is as bad as what I have seen in Courcelette, I would not wish my worst enemy to go there."[17] The fourth verse contains one of the few references to poison gas which

I have found in local poets' work. "Star shells", when exploded in the sky at night, would illuminate "no-man's land".

The internal rhyme in this poem suggests that Halley had read Robert Service's work. (His popular *Spell of the Yukon and Other Verses* had been published in 1907.)

Afterwards

The battle's over now. The regiments stand
*   Shattered and worn upon the ridge they've won.*
Staring with weary eyes o'er "No Man's Land,"
*   Clouded in smoke which masks the morning sun,*
Praying a quick relief may come before
*   Endurance dies, and they can fight no more.*

A silence settles down o'er the battle ground.
*   The brazen voices of the guns are still*
Tho' every breach contains a waiting round
*   Eager to scream across the captured hill,*
To headlong hurl the hostile legions back
*   And crumble to the dust their fierce attack.*

The battle's over now, the joy bells peal,
*   And all thro' Britain's Empire hand clasps hand;*
The platform speakers praise our wall of steel;
*   Hysteric crowds cheer madly thro' the land.*
But could they see the ground that we have won,
*   They'd cease their cheering e'er they well begun.*

Blackened and scarred, scorched by a poisoned breath,
*   Stand remnants of a forest dead and still.*
Nothing could live before the hand of death
*   Which fell with dread precision on the hill*
And other forms in grey and khaki dressed
*   Lie 'neath the trees in never-ending rest.*

Crater joins crater where the great shells came,
*   Amid the tangled wire and liquid mud,*
Where ruined villages still smoke and flame,

And streamlets turn to pools of slime and blood.
While here and there, its day of warfare done,
Half hid in earth there lies a shattered gun.

Look near the forts that drown the captured hill,
Mixed with the clay and trampled in the mire,
Small grim-faced heaps are lying stiff and still,
Caught by the blast of dread machine gun fire;
They fell a ripened harvest to the gun,
And every man is some poor mother's son.

But watch the ridge: a sudden movement there;
A hushed expectancy that one can feel
As tho' some mighty voice had cried "Beware!"
See from the hostile trench a gleam of steel,
Then high above a brilliant rocket soars,
And down between the lines the barrage roars.

Gone is the silence—nerve destroying screams
Herald the shells which hurtle thro' the air;
Columns of mud spout up in fan-shaped streams,
Splinters of steel are shrieking everywhere,
While powder smoke, a reeking, dusky pall,
Falls like a great drop curtain over all.

Thro' the dense fog the rifle bullets whine;
Rattling machine guns hurl their leaden rain:
Wave after wave breaks on the thinning line,
Rolling away to form and charge again,
While thro' this hellish music loudly runs
The never ending thunder of the guns.

Crowded and close the wavering advance
Crouches to bursts of shrapnel overhead.
Down thro' their ranks the high explosives dance.
Hell's imps and outcasts dancing for the dead,
All wreathed in smoke that ghoulish ballet there,
Mocks these poor wrecks who lie too still to care.

Grumbling and slow the thunder dies away
Like some gorged beast by slaughter satisfied.

Slowly the smoke lifts and the light of day
    Floods to the ridge where countless men have died.
Look, you of England, see them lying there,
    Stout, stalwart sons your Empire ill could spare.

See for once that sight and conscience bids you pause.
    Think for yourself and never mind your cheers;
What can you do to aid your country's cause;
    How can you help to dry your Empire's tears.
So give y our all for nothing less will do;
    Think of those dead who gave their all for you.

(*Colonist*, 13 March 1918, 10)

Late in the war, Halley still uses the traditional, poetic contractions such as "o'er", and words such as "legions". Living on Salt Spring Island, yet he speaks of England, still imbued with an imperial patriotism which the *Colonist* editors found admirable. However, the poem comes closer than almost any other piece of verse published in Victoria during the Great War to giving a real sense of a modern battlefield. Despite the persistence of high diction, moreover, Halley's poem is near to revealing a disillusionment with the nature of war and a sincere desire to communicate its reality. Was there a turning point for Halley? For James Pedley, it was the death of his best friend, John Gordon, by the bullet of a sniper: "Up to that fatal morning the war had been pageantry to me sometimes interesting, sometimes stupid, but always a sort of Lord Mayor's show that you looked at and made jokes about. Of a sudden I was made to realize that war is terrible, too terrible."[18]

Obviously, Halley believes that soldiers must fight on and civilians must support them through War Loans. In neither of his poems quoted here, however, does he refer to Canada, and this in March 1918; i.e. after the Battle of Vimy Ridge, when Canadians were said to have achieved a new sense of national identity.

The reference to blood oozing in the trenches and shell-craters may be poetic exaggeration. The redness noticed there was probably due to some species of small protozoan lying in the puddles.[19]

Robert Valentine Harvey

Marching Song
(At Valcartier Camp, Québec)

We're going to the front, boys, to the bloody fields of war,
The fields where fought our fathers in the grand old days
    of yore;
We'll fight as once our fathers did at Crécy and Poitiers,
The Eighty-Eighth, the Eighty-Eighth Victoria Fusiliers.

Where once we fought the Frenchmen, like brothers now
    we stand
To drive the hated Prussians from out the smiling land;
We'll help them pull his palace about the Kaiser's ears,
The Eighty-Eighth, the Eighty-Eighth Victoria Fusiliers.

We'll see those gallant regiments whose fame shall never
    die,
Whose colors tell the story of courage proud and high;
And when we fight beside them, there'll be no doubts or
    fears,
In the Eighty-Eighth, the Eighty-Eighth Victoria Fusiliers.

Now England pledged her honor to a nation weak and
    small,
'Twas but a "scrap of paper," but her honor's all in all;
So that is why they send for us, through young we be in
    years,
The Eighty-Eigthth, the Eighty-Eighth Victoria Fusiliers.

And when the war is over, and we see our homes once more
We'll tell again the story of the part we bore in war;
And proudly spread our colors, and give three hearty
    cheers,
For the Eighty-Eighth, the Eighty-Eighth Victoria Fusiliers.

(*Colonist,* 16 September 1914, 4)

The treaty which recognized Belgium's neutrality was referred to by the German chancellor as a "scrap of paper". This poem, redolent of the optimism of 1914, uses the American spellings of "colors" and "honor". The accepted "Canadian" spellings (with a "u") did not become common until after the war.

Thomas A. Hollins

British Columbia

*You can sing of "Way Down South" till you're foaming at
    the mouth.
You can howl "Down Texas Way", for all I care.
You can yell "The Marseillaise" for the balance of your
    days,
Or "Uber Ober Alles", if you dare.
Let Pat sing "Tipperary" till we all are sick and weary.
Let the Yankee sing "My Country 'Tis of Thee".
After all is said and done, the best country 'neath the sun
Is the province of old B.C.*

*No "Down South" but "Farthest West" is the bravest and
    the best.
Where the broad Pacific rolls so grand and free.
Stream and forest, mountain range, fruit and flowers,
    wold and grange
Reach perfection in the Province of B.C.*

*The province of B.C., that's where I long to be.
The home of all that's beautiful and fearless and free,
From Alaska to the Bound'ry, from the Rockies to the sea.
As fair a place as Paradise, the province of B.C.*

*You may seek the whole world over, but you cannot match
    Vancouver.
Okanagan is the garden of the Lord.
Victoria is a shrine both human and divine
With Esquimalt standing sentinel and guard.*

The roses shine in Picardy and apples blooms in Normandy.
B.C. has apple blooms and roses, too,
Mighty rivers and cascades, silver springs and forest glades,
While Italy cannot beat a sky so blue.

The Province of B.C., that's where I long to be.
The home of all that's beautiful and fearless and free.
From Alaska to the Bound'ry, from the Rockies to the sea.
A fairer place than Paradise, the province of B.C.

(*Colonist*, 19 October 1918, 4)

George V. Jarvis

Thoughts of Hone

It often makes me homesick,
When the sun goes down in the west,
Casting its rays in my dugout door
Sinking behind a crest.

As I sit on my bunk alone
And my thoughts begin to roam
With my brow buried deep in my hands
I'm thinking of those at home.

Thinking so hard that it seems a dream
And I think I am home again
'Til I hear the roar of a Fritzy shell
Like that of an express train.

Then again I begin to realize
What it is to be at war.
And I see the flashes of the battle front
As I stand in the dugout door.

Of course it sets one thinking
Living in a place like this
And dodging whizbangs night and day,
As they pass you with a hiss.

It's not just one, it's millions
Who are out for the same big kick.
To overthrow the Kaiser
And all the Hindenburg clique.

Now of course, they take some beating.
So we are out here doing our bits
Packing ammunition up to the guns
And sending it over to Fritz.

I can tell you this is no easy task
When a moke you've got to guide
With mud and water to your neck
Then into a shellhole you slide.

We only wish this war would end
So we could homeward roam.
With loving arms out stretched to greet us,
Home Sweet Home.

(Muriel Jarvis Ackinclose, *For the Love of George* [Victoria: First Choice, 89].)

Not verse of the quality one might expect from Keats or Browning, Ted Hughes or Philip Larkin, nevertheless this poem is evidence of the high degree of literacy in Victoria's working class a century ago. Jarvis just hints at some of the miseries he's experienced at the front. He, too, seems to have hoped for "regime change" in Germany. A "moke" was a worn-out horse, a nag or a donkey. Later, Jarvis recuperated at Resthaven Hospital, perhaps in the company of Edwin Freeman, another Victoria soldier-poet.

R.F.L.

To the Jubilee

We lie in our cots at the Jubilee [Hospital]
and think of the days gone by.
We dream and stare at the ceilings bare,
As we used to gaze at the sky.

There are no star shells or Verey lights
Aloft in the still night air,
Though the starlight shines in our Nurses' eyes,
As they tend us with loving care.

It's a long, long time to look back to
In that brave old land of France;
It sometimes seems to be but a dream
That has passed, like a fleeting glance,
And the Flanders cold, or the Eastern steam,
But the vague review of a trance.

Some lost a leg, or an arm,
And some an eye or a hand,
But we're home at last, and safe from harm,
A happy, though battered, band.
And we cling to life and its wondrous charm,
And laugh at Old Death's cold hand.

We certainly have our share of the luck
To be here after where we've been,
Instead, as our Pals, with their grit and pluck
Gone West to the Great Unseen.
No joy ride theirs, in their Blighty truck,
But a cross on their bedspreads green.

So here good luck to the Jubilee, Boys,
To our Doctors, Matrons and Nurses,
May their lives be long with earthly joys,
And free from war's cares and curses.
But, for fear they'll bid me cease my noise
I'd better close these verses.

Well, there's just one thought before I stop,
May we never forget their care;
When we get outside, if we can but hop
Let's help them and do our share,
For we know full well the Hospital Shop
Can't run all the time on air.

Jubilee Hospital, February 1919.
(*Colonist,* 16 February, 1919, 9)

The hospital's name commemorates the Golden Jubilee of Queen Victoria (1887). Verey lights were flares shot from pistols. At Resthaven Hospital, Freeman expressed similar feelings which must have been widespread among wounded veterans. "Gone West" was a popular euphemism for having been killed in action.

W.P.M.

Say the Word

> Britain has a painful task, in honor bound to do,
> And when her honor is at stake, she fights and sees it through.
> Each British possession hears and answers Britain's call,
> Knowing, as sons to a mother, they owe their very all.
>
> As Canada owes the Motherland help in time of need,
> Each Province has its share to pay in money, men and
>   deed;
> Each city, town and parish owes that province, too,
> In comparison to the size, all the good that it can do.
>
> Breathes there a man with soul so dead in Victoria,
> Who can offer no manly excuse for not enlisting today?
> Who denies this fair city the honor that we crave,
> And hides away in darkness in terror of the grave.
>
> Come, ye men of honor: come, ye men of fame;
> Join your city regiment and banish fear and shame.
> Your King and country need you. Can you hear the call?
> Then come—don't tarry—say the word—that's all.

(*Colonist,* 27 November 1915, 5)

The verse of "W.P.M." (a member of the 88th Regiment) is a good example of the early idealism and imperial patriotism which prevailed in Victoria. Like many of his generation, this anonymous soldier-poet knew the English classics, for he paraphrases "The Lay of the Last Minstrel" by Sir Walter Scott (1771-1832) which includes the lines,

Breathes there the man with soul so dead
Who never to himself hath said,
This is my own, my native land!

Earl Marling

Dream of a Canadian Soldier on the Archangel Front

Corporal Jack from his bed rose early one morn;
To me he looked disturbed and somewhat worn;
Quite out of the ordinary his tone did seem.
His great distress was caused by this strange dream.

Peace had been declared and war was over at last,
Stilled forever was the war-bugle's loud blast.
The war-worn soldier had returned to his home
And resolved never from his loved ones to roam.

Canadian troops all had returned from France,
Everyone proved that they had taken their chance.
Flags flew gaily, loud cheered the throng;
Great was their welcome as they smartly marched along.

At Valcartier camp they, heroes all, collected.
This famous spot was by Sir Sam selected.
All the branches and the units of the Corps
Prepared for review as never before.

Each man was checked with exactitude and care.
They made certain that all the men were there;
Reviewed by the chiefs of our happy land,
Proud to represent such a fighting band.

Quite suddenly General Currie's face grew dark
And to Sir Robert he made this remark;
"Canadians to Russia were sent some years ago;
What happened to them? Does anyone know?"

Strange to relate, no one said a word;
As to their fate nothing was ever heard;
Sir Robert then replied: "Of them I never thought.
That brigade, unfortunately, we have forgot."

Delegates were sent to that far distant land
To search and enquire for that ill-fated band;
But enquire as they might from every source,
Not a trace could be found of that fighting force.

After years of waiting they agreed to disband,
Each and all to settle on the land.
Years rolled by, their fate remained a mystery.
Of them no mention could found in history.

They now know how to wield the Russian axe,
Thresh peas, make boots, and spin the crops of flax.
The only time you will hear English spoken
Is when they ask for some "tobacco smokum".

This is the dream as it was told to me
It's got me guessing what our fate shall be;
And now I wonder, and perhaps you wonder too,
If such dreams as this, ever do come true.

(*Colonist,* 10 June 1919, 8)

"Sir Sam" is a reference to the Minister of Militia and Defence. "Sir Robert" was Robert Borden (1854-1937), prime minister from 1911 to 1920.

Loftus MacInnes

The Cynics

How often have we heard the cynics prate
Of our proud empire toppling in decay,
Our youth grown sickly and degenerate
And valour with our grandsires passed away.
How they would mark with supercilious air
The silken hose the monocle or ties
Of lurid hue that foppish youngsters wear,
And from such weighty evidence surmise
That manhood and virility were sped
With the black coats of dour Victorian days

That loyalty and sacrifice were dead
While each his own gain sought in selfish ways:—
The men who fell upon the fields of Flanders
Have answered well the sneer of cynic slanders.

(*Canadian Poems of the Great War,* 131)

Born in Victoria in 1891, McInnes attended McGill University and in 1914 joined the Department of Indian Affairs in Ottawa. In October 1915, he married the daughter of the poet Archibald Lampman. He does not seem to have served in the Great War, but this poem expresses both imperial patriotism and a positive view of that conflict. He died in 1952.

George Redhead

While We're Marching through Siberia . . .
(Song for the S.S.E.F.)

Our men come from the sunny South
And from the State of Maine
With veterans from the western front
Back in the fight again.
We'll start the grand offensive
While singing this refrain:
When we're marching through Siberia.

Hurrah, Hurrah, we're Western to the core.
Hurrah, Hurrah, we're at home on any shore.
We'll whip the Bolshevikis
And then we'll ask for more,
While we march through Siberia.

We're miners from the far Yukon
And cowboys from the plain.
We've heard the call of British blood
Our freedom to retain.
We've always done your duty and
We'll do it once again.
While we're marching through Siberia.

We're sailing o'er the Western Sea
   Out towards the setting sun,
With a single thought in mind:
   To go and get the Hun.
We'll wipe'm clean right off the map
   With bayonet and gun.
When we've marched through Siberia.

"Written by a boy at Willows, a private in the Siberian force."
(*Colonist,* 2 October 1918, 17)

The misplaced idealism of 1914 was still alive at the war's end, for here a young man is willing to risk his life for the vague concept of "freedom", which was not always clearly defined. Typically, he also conflates the "Huns" and the Bolsheviks.

James Robertson

A Grouch

Is there any more need
For this drill of the Swede?
And we're wearing of polishing buttons,
   It gives us the pip;
Why not let all that rip?
We're keen to be ripping up Teutons.

(*The Western Scot,* 4 December 1915, 6)

As we have seen, other soldier-poets felt the same way about training.

"Swedish Drill" was a form of physical exercise popular at the time.

Poultice Wallopers

We're only "Poultice Wallopers", a-bringing up the rear,
A-picking up the step that's lost between the band and here;

And when we're out upon the "Route" we aye can raise a cheer
As we go marching on.

No! we are not downhearted,
No! we are not downhearted,
No! we are not downhearted,
As we go marching on.

We're only "Poultice Wallopers", a-bringing up the rear,
And at the Diarrhoea Squad" you sometime throw a jeer.
But how about that "No. 8" when you were feeling queer?
As we go marching on.

We're only "Poultice Wallopers" a-bringing up the rear;
But in prompt "first aid" or at "sick parade", when your
works are out of gear,
You bless the "No. 9" that cured effects of last night's beer,
As we go marching on.

We're only "Poultice Wallopers" a-bringing up the rear;
But with fractured bones or blistered heels you're pleased
to have us near;
You'll want our splint and bandages before another year,
As we go marching on.

We're only "Poultice Wallopers" a-bringing up the rear;
We can't enjoy the martial strains that cheer the Pioneer;
But we'll be there in step, my boys, without a doubt or fear,
When we get to Berlin.

No! we are not downhearted,
No! we are not downhearted,
No! we are not downhearted,
As we go marching on.

(*The Western Scot,* 4 December 1915, 6)

The term "poultice walloper" originated in British naval slang for medical staff. Clearly, Robertson had the widespread confidence that Canada and its allies would eventually conquer Berlin.

Lorne Ross

At Peace

The calm of summer's evening
    Falls soft on the slender mound,
While drooping flowers swaying
    Waft sweet incense from the ground.

Peaceful at rest he slumbers,
    Who fought for the Cause he loved,
One of the countless numbers
    For Freedom to shed his blood.

He heard the voice of Empire
    Sound clear on Alaska's height,
Calling her sons from afar
    To join the righteous fight.

Where sweeps the mighty Yukon
    Through the land of eternal snow,
He sprang to the help of Britain
    In battle against the foe.

He followed Duty's guidance
    O'er wide continent and sea,
To the blood-stained field of France
    Where men battled to be free.

Amid the ruin and carnage,
    The thunder of gun and shell,
Facing grim death with courage
    Fearless he fought and fell.

There where night's benediction
    Breathes quiet o'er the silent sod,
Waiting the bless'd resurrection
    He rests in peace with his God.

(Canada in Khaki, vol. II, 172)

It is hard to know if Ross is referring to a specific soldier such as a Western Scot here, but his vocabulary and imagery are typical. Death is "slumber" in exquisitely beautiful surroundings; the enemy is "the foe". The illusion that every soldier was "fearless" is evident.

Ross was a soldier, but his poem opens with one of the most popular euphemisms used by civilians: the notion that the soldier killed in action is merely sleeping peacefully. The image occurs in poems by other soldiers, too, but much less frequently. The poem is another catalog of the values and ideals which many soldier-poets were encouraged to uphold such as the sense of a "righteous" crusade in defence of "Freedom" and "Duty".

The Western Scots

The strong came forth from the farthest North,
    From the Yukon's frozen shore;
From the western side of the Great Divide,
    From south of the "Fifty-four".

From working the mine and felling the pine,
    They have come at the Empire's call.
They have dropped their packs in the Caribou tracks
    And willing left it all.

They have hunted the bear in his darkest lair,
    And tracked through the woods and snows;
Through the heat and rain they have ridden the plain,
    In the south where the Kootenay flows.

In the Empire's need it is men of this breed
    Who furnish a bulwark of strength,
And the Hunnish hate and the Belgian fate
    From England hold at length.

For, deadly the shot of the Western Scot
    When fired at the German foe,
And fearful the feel of his shining steel,
    As the Hunnish hordes shall know.

> *With eager eye and head held high,*
> *They will leap through the wire-blocked trench,*
> *With the courage fine of the British line*
> *And the lightsome heart of the French.*
>
> *The Germans will sense their impotence*
> *To grapple the men of this breed;*
> *In a stand-up fight and a test of might*
> *'Tis more than culture they'll need.*
>
> *So here's to the day when we join the fray,*
> *To play our part in the game;*
> *And before we are hit may we do our bit*
> *To add to the Empire's Fame.*

(*The Western Scot,* 2 February 1916, 9, and *The Western Scot Commemorative Edition,* 1917, 30.)

The Western Scots (67th Battalion) left Victoria on 26 March 1916 for Europe. When this was published, Ross had already served in France, but service at the front had not dulled his taste for traditional rhetoric. His imperial patriotism is also evident but, ironically, the Germans used similar vocabulary to justify their cause, for they believed that they were defending their culture or way of life (their *Kultur*) from a conspiracy of encircling enemies which also meant that their *Freiheit* (freedom) was threatened.

On the theme of Canadian soldiers coming from the rugged north, see also Leonard McLeod Gould's description of the men from Comox-Atlin which, although partly true, contributed to the notion that all Canadian soldiers were rugged outdoorsmen, which they most certainly were not.

C.B. Schreiber

Sabaid

We win the fight, so fear not Death,
    We battle for a principle, a cause.
With sinking body, fading breath,
    Still press ye on without a pause—
        "Sabaid."

Struggling hand to hand, or, like a beast,
    Snarling and biting—"seeing red"—
Glorying in brute strength and ghoulish feast
    Till finally we kill—"He's dead—
        Sabaid".

Count not the lives of comrades lost
    Who come not back from out the strife
They gave their all—nor counted cost
    In Death, they've justified their life.
        "Sabaid."

When at the last our aims are ended;
    Our hopes, our aspirations all attained,
Mind at rest, and bodies mended
    We'll say—halt, blind and maimed—
        "Sabaid".

And if in this never-ending gluttony of blood,
    You find your death, from Hand on High—
A grain of sand to stem a flood—
    Exulting to the last, still wc cry
        "Sabaid".

(*The Western Scot Commemorative Edition*, 1917, 38)

    "Sabaid" is Gaelic for "fight to the finish". The unusual poem is realistic, but never actually says what the "cause" is! (Presumably all his readers knew . . .)

Ralf Sheldon-Williams

The False Focus
(Concerning the "Girls' White Feather Brigade",
with apologies to the late Robert Browning.)

Just for a little white feather he left us,
Just for a "favor" they stuck in his coat.
One foolish fad of a man hath bereft us
While silly girl-children giggle and gloat.
They that had love to give doled him out pity;
Gave one more twist to the hat-pin of spite;
Piled the last straw when they thought to be witty;
Sent a man wrong when he knew what was right.

So the soiled honor and violate pride of him
Dodged every mean and malevolent eye;
Flinched from each whisper or chuckle not meant for him,
As another brat born of the first idle lie.
Who guesses he yearned to the glitter of battle
Even while duty chose the drab path to be trod.
Here's just one spoiled life more, one more broken rattle,
One heart robbed of manhood, one soul robbed of God!

Victoria, September 7, 1915.

(*Colonist*, 8 September 1915, 2)

In August 1914, British Admiral Charles Fitzgerald founded the Order of the White Feather "of Shame", which encouraged women to give out white feathers to young men who had apparently not enlisted. Some young Canadian women followed suit. Sheldon-Williams enlisted in February 1916.

The reference to Robert Browning concerns his poem, "The Lost Leader", which begins "Just for a handful of silver he left us/Just for a riband to stick in his coat" and laments the growing conservatism of the poet William Wordsworth.

Letters from Home

(10th Canadian Machine Gun Co., B.E.F. France, 1917)

*You say such nice things in your letters, you dear people
    who write from Home,*
*Had we time we'd be getting swelled-headed over here
    on the silly old Somme,*
*We look and long for a letter and say bad words when
    there's none,*
*While the A.P.O. earns our best blessing if it only chucks
    out the one.*
*Yes, we look and we long for your letters—but somehow,
    you know, it's queer—*
*But the delight they give is a mixed one, the joy they give
    is too dear.*
*For we're men while we're fooling out here, dears, if we
    never were men before,*
*And men must be men all the time, dears, when they're
    fooling about with war.*

*And perhaps we resent it a little that you add to our daily
    "fatigue"—*
*Or is it the ration candle and the dug-out draught are in
    league*
*To make such a job of the reading of these simple letters
    from you—*
*To make them blurry and smudgy—to make us just a bit
    blue?*
*Yet I'd swear there's something else in it—I'd hate to ask
    any chap,*
*But I bet if I yelled "Cry-Baby!" there's some one would
    collar the cap!*
*Yes, they're simple enough, your letters, yet they say the
    deuce of a lot,*
*And we smother that frog-in-the-throat by making the
    tongue say "Rot!"*

*You see, we're just doing our job, dears—don't make it
    the harder to do*
*By saying such nice things about us in the letters that
    come from you.*

We're just doing our silly old job here—a giddy old daily
     round
Of fatigue and patrol and etceteras such as "getting to
     know your ground";
With just now and then a spasm—you might almost call
     it a thrill—
Which takes us out of the common-or-garden grind of the
     mill

And makes us one with the star-shell—disembodied,
     radiant, clean,
Till we come back to earth like a dud, with a prayer that
     we haven't been seen
By some fool who's just as foolish as ourselves in his
     "crowded hour",
And just as wise as we are when it's the other man's turn
     to "tower".

So don't make us one of the heroes, the johnnies the
     sages sing—
Why! All of us love our fooling and the chance to have
     our fling,
To play at this glorified "footer", to get just the fun we
     need—
Still—a letter each week if you can, dears—
Never mind if they're hard to read!

(*Names Like Trumpets*, 11-12)

The self-deprecating tone and the minimizing of war's hazards was part of soldiers' self-censorship. His reference to the duties of the male is typical, but he is aware of misleading romantic rhetoric about "heroes". Sheldon Williams also expresses a sense of identity with German enemy. He is one of the few Victoria soldier—poets who wrote positively about their war experience.

Runners of the Somme
(Somewhere in France 1917)

They didn't pull off any grand-stand play;
They seldom did much in the gallery way;
They were generally dirty and sometimes shaved,
But never the flag of their country waved.
Because they weren't just built that way.
There wasn't much that they had to say
Unless it was on the subject of pay,
Which amounted to quite a franc a day—
Not enough, you'll admit to marry on—
But they packed in their pouch when out of a mooch
What's better than any brand of "hootch"—
The motto, or badge, or what you please,
Which in army circles is quite the "wheeze"—
The thing we call "Carry on!"

They'd grouch as every good soldier should,
But they treated their job as if sawing wood.
They took their turn as they took their rum,
Without blast of bugle or tuck of drum
They knew, each hour, what they had to face
But it never struck them to slacken pace
Through "three by night and three by day"
Must read the toll of their urgent way,
Which often looked good to tarry on
Because of the mud
Or a neighbourly dud,
Or a noise not a little bit like a dud.
They'd light up another wierd issue fag
A "'Alf a Mo'" or a "Regent or "Flag"—
And cheerfully "Carry on!"

They'd give the foot-slogger their simple praise,
With no need for their own "laborious days".
They guessed that the heroes at the gun
Thought small potatoes of those who "run".
But some Persons saw and made a note
And when they had time sat down and wrote
In terms that astounded the blushing runner—

Not to mention the past-pluperfect gunner—
On the subject of how to "Carry on",
And took as a model
The ceaseless toddle—
In mud-time ludicrously like a waddle—
That's now the fashion wherever you go
Because the brass hats have made it so—
We call it the "Carry on!"

(*Names Like Trumpets,* 13)

Leonard McLeod Gould also praised "The Runners" (of the 102nd Canadian Infantry Battalion). (See above)

D.B. Shepherd

A Query from the Recruit

We like your charming city
    On this soft Pacific slope,
When our Eastern snap is over,
    We'll come again, we hope.
We love your snow-capped mountains,
    Each city, street and lane,
But tell me, some old resident,
    Does it always, always, rain?

The soldier from the eastland
    You've received with open arms,
Till we, though bound for Russian snows
    Forget the war's alarms.
We're in the Golden West now,
    And we're awfully glad we came,
But tell me, some old-timer,
    Does it always, always, rain?

Your climate's not so very bad,
It might be worse, we know;
We might be freezing in our tents,
And drilling in the snow.
But e'er we leave we'd like to see
The sunshine once again,
So tell me please, and tell me now,
Does it always, always, rain?

P.S. Dear Mr. Editor,—I would make this a lot longer but the sheet anchor of my tent is adrift and we are going full speed for Fort Street with breakers ahead.
(Times, 14 December 1918, 7)

Mud seems to have been endemic in the Willows training camp. In January 1918, **a** *Times* journalist reported that "the recent copious rains [have] made quagmires over which it has been necessary to throw boards down so as to prevent the men imagining they were already in Flanders in winter time" (4 January 1918, 4). [Fig.II.7.2] Rifleman Shepherd's complaint elicited a response from Rifleman D. Macksen, of the 260th Battalion Canadian Rifles, who pointed out that at least Shepherd was not standing knee-deep in snow as he would have been in Ontario or for that matter in France, where Canadians had to endure much more than rainfall (*Times,* 19 December 1918, 6). However, Will Bird records that, during the November rains in the trenches, "our feet were always soggy, and some of the men were on the verge of becoming despondent."[20]

In France, Robert Service understood this. In his "Rhymes of a Red Cross Man", he wrote "Song of the Winter Weather", which includes the lines,

It isn't the bounce of the bombs
That gives us a positive pain:
It's the strafing we get
When the weather is wet—
It's the RAIN,
RAIN,
RAIN.[21]

Cecil W. Tildesley

The Telephonist-O-Pip

When they're "mixing 'em" (already you have got your
*   gas-mask on)*
*   And the other kind are bursting pretty near;*
When ev'ry one is calling up at ev'ry plug at once
*   With persistent iteration loud and clear;*
When you've got a stack of messages, the urgent ones on
*   top,*
*   And Brigade's become sarcastic at delay—*
And the one and only candle left sucks up its final drop,
*   And you're left in dreary darkness and dismay;*
Then the great thing to remember, and of course you
*   won't forget,*
*   Is the need of cool and calm insouciance.*
With that clear and balanced judgment which has never
*   failed you yet,*
*   You act upon a rapid mental glance,*
You grasp that good revolver—meant for such a pass as
*   this—*
*   And point it at your "window-of-the-soul",*
You press the giddy trigger—mechanics does the rest—
*   And take up the peaceful job of shov'ling coal.*

(*Times*, 10 October 1917, 16)

An observation or field artillery post was known as an "O. Pip", but in this case the telephonist could have had "one pip"; i.e. he could have been a lieutenant. Whatever his rank, his work was often critical to the success of an attack. To prevent telephone lines from being cut by shell fire, they were often buried as much as seven feet underground or ran through underground tunnels. At Vimy Ridge, many miles of telephone line connected the Canadian and British trenches.

Suicides at the front were not unknown, as Morton and Granatstein have pointed out.[22] Robert Service describes a soldier trapped and dying on barbed wire in no-man's land.

> *The man whom I heard [moaning] is dead.*
> *Now I understand:*
> *A bullet hole in his head,*
> *A pistol gripped in his hand.*
> *Well, he knew what to do—*
> *Yes, and now I know too . . .*[23]

J. L. Vallie

To Joe

> *Well done, old boy! From one less worthy, hail!*
> *Thy trials are over, passed beyond the veil.*
> *The great reward is thine. Let thy youth's friend*
> *Thy life and noble sacrifice commend.*
> *A sportsman always, worthy of the name.*
> *A clear, consistent player of the game.*
> *And when the strife is o'er, the victory won,*
> *May Canada be proud of such a son.*
> *And in the land thou gave thy life to save*
> *May alien hands deck reverently thy grave.*

(*Times,* 21 December 1917, 4)

Vallie was a patient at the former naval hospital in Esquimalt. This "Disabled Soldiers Re-establishment Hospital" had been adapted by the Military Hospitals Commission to serve recuperating veterans. Joseph Gorman, originally from Ottawa, and serving with the Royal Naval Air Service, was a sports reporter for the Victoria *Times.* He was twenty-eight years old when he was killed.

Edward M.B. Vaughan

Canada
(England, October 1) [1916]

You may boast of merrie England
With her roses red and white.
You may sing of Scotland's glory
From early morn 'til night.
But the joys of hope and freedom
You can't begin to tell
Unless you've been in Canada
And learned her witching spell.

The ancient bards of Erin
They sing of clashing blades
To Tara's lofty chieftains
And Ulster's blue-eyed maids.
But they never knew the dangers
Of Ypres' heroic line
Or saw Canadian soldiers
Press on through shell and mine.

Oh! Scotland's hills are bonny
And Scotland's maids are fair
And with bonnie Annie Laurie
There's none that can compare,
Save by foaming Western rivers
And soft Acadian vales
Or lofty cloud-capped mountains
That dwarf the hills of Wales.
Our maple's autumn glory
Is known the world around.
In broad Canadian valleys
The fairest maids are found.
Hail to our wide Dominion!
Long may she reign supreme!
The envy of the nations,
The patriot's deathless theme.

(*Times*, 24 October 1916, 13)

Vaughan's work is a rare example of Canadian patriotism in local soldier-poets' verse. Typically of a Victoria poet, however, he compares Canada to the British Isles. Exactly which geo-political entity the Canadian soldier was asked to defend, however, was sometimes vague as Fig. III.4 suggests.

Fig.III.4: "Not Everyone Can Fight for the Preservation of the British Empire. All Can Be Loyal and Patriotic: Support the Patriotic Fund". Parts of Central Canada and the Atlantic provinces may resemble this image, but it looks nothing like the typical landscapes of the Prairies or British Columbia. For many civilian or enlisted Victorians, however, its resemblance to England was appropriate. (*Colonist*, 22 July 1917, 12)

Strawberry Jam
A message from the trenches to the jam makers of Canada by the late Edward M.B. Vaughan C.E.F. who was recently killed in action.

> *They feed us on Apricot, Citron and Plum,*
> *But what has become of the Strawberry Jam?*
> *It comes from Australia and Canada too,*
> *From England and Scotland in varying hue;*
> *They give us a tin between six and for-seven,*

Or if you're unlucky it may be eleven.
For citron or damson we don't give—ahem,—
But what has become of the Strawberry Jam?

There's an army of transport that tends to the mules.
Are they playing the game by a straight set of rules?
There's the Officer's Mess and the Hospital Corps—
There's an army in England won't come to the war—
Is the answer we seek concealed among these?
Last year in the world did all Strawberries freeze?
We's [sic] sated with marmalade, apple and plum,
Oh? What has become of the Strawberry Jam?

They ask us to carry the war to an end,
Till the knees of the Prussian shall bend.
They feed us on bully beef, biscuit and plum,
And yet they deny us that Strawberry Jam.
Unkind is the most we term such abuse;
We grouse and we grumble but what is the use?
Now answer my question kind friends, if you can.
Oh! What has become of that Strawberry Jam?

Have the Strawberry growers all gone to the war?
Has an order been issued to raise them no more?
Perhaps they consider it bad for our health,
Perhaps they's [sic] condemned as superfluous wealth.
Of plum there's a plenty or else it is tar.
The export of apple Australia should bar.
Now what is the answer—pray tell if you can—
Oh! What has become of the Strawberry Jam?

We've plenty of bully beef, biscuits and tea,
We get enough cheese for to block up the sea;
We shave in the marmalade tins by the score;
The sight of a bean tin no more we can bear.
We've bacon for breakfast and butter for tea,
Yet still there's a question arises to me—
To build of the bully a dugout we plan—
But what has become of the Strawberry Jam?

(*Colonist, 19 July 1917, 4*)

The First C.E.F.

They rose at honor's bidding
To save the land from shame.
Their names shall live forever
On Britain's roll of fame.
Their limbs were torn and shattered
By German shot and shell.

Yet still their spirit triumphs
Though strewn in heaps they fell.
For every fallen hero
A hundred bayonets shine,
To guard our red cross banner
On many a hard fought line.
The crimson banners swelling
On every wind that blows
Hold firm the cause of Freedom
Against unnumbered foes.

Hail to the deathless heroes!
The first to draw the blade;
Their lives and homes and loved ones
On Freedom's altars laid.
They rose at honor's bidding
To save the land from shame.
Their names shall live forever
On Britain's roll of fame.

(*Times,* 4 August 1917, 7)

Even in 1917 (although the poem could have been written earlier), Vaughan still seemed to admire the sense of adventure and romance which motivated many early volunteers. He has the same romantic attachment to the bayonet ("the blade") that Armstrong possessed. In his semi-autobiographical novel, Peregrine Acland describes his protagonist as yearning for "romance" and seeks it working as a cowboy in Alberta. "Brought up among books, he wished to develop . . . as an adventurer, a man of action . . ."[24] So probably did Vaughan and many of his contemporaries. Vaughan, however, allows his readers to know something of the reality of the war. Victoria's soldiers' arms and legs "were torn and shattered" and they fall "strewn in heaps". Such descriptions reflect the point made by Ian Hugh Maclean Miller, that Torontonians, at least, were under few illusions about the grisliness of trench combat.[25]

Vaughan's use of the word "heroes" raises the question of whether or not such terms are now devoid of meaning. What did the word mean then—and what does it mean today? Were all Canadian soldiers heroes? What is heroism? In 2006 Kenneth Radley wrote, "The very word 'hero' is fast becoming meaningless, if it is not already. Away from the battlefield, it should apply only in the most exceptional circumstances; even in reference to the battlefield it should be used sparingly."[26]

Ralph Younghusband

1914-1917 The Litany of the Trenches

> *By the thunder of the guns*
> *And the cruelties of the Huns*
> *On the weak, defenceless ones;*
> *Avenge our daughters and our sons!*
>   *Hear us, holy Jesu!*

> *Bless our loved ones far away,*
> *Grant, oh, grant dear Lord, that they*
> *May return to us some day!*
> *Hear us when for them we pray:*
>   *Spare them, holy Jesu!*

> *By the shrapnel's stinging drench,*
> *On Belgians, British and on French*
> *In the sodden, reeking trench*
> *And the powder's sickening stench!*
>   *Hear us, holy Jesu!*

By the women left forlorn,
Waiting weeping in the dawn
By their dear ones bruised and torn!
Jesus! Comfort all who mourn!
  Hear them, holy Jesu!

Lead us on to victory,
Through these days of agony!
Set the Allied nations free
From brutal Prussian tyranny.
  Save them, holy Jesu!

Saviour, called the Prince of Peace,
To the prisoners bring release
Before their miseries increase!
Let this dreadful slaughter cease!
  Hear us holy Jesu!

(*Colonist,* 21 March 1917, 4)

To India

Dedicated with respect and admiration to
Lieut.-Col. Sir Francis Younghusband,
KCIE, KCSI, author, explorer and soldier

("OM-SATCHIT-EKAM-BRAHMA!")

> *Mother of warrior sons!*
> *When the call went forth from the East,*
> *Like ravens unto a feast*
> *You sent them swift to the fray*
> *Who know how to fight and pray*
> *At home or under the guns.*
> *Mother of warrior sons!*
> *Who are turbaned, subtle and calm*
> *Full of the mystical charm*
> *Of Shiva, Krishna amd Brahm,*
> *Who know that death is a gate*
> *Opening to endless life!*

They welcomed the hour of strife
And smiled at the stings of fate
Mother of warrior sons!

Sacred! Ancient on earth,
Filled with the glamour of things
That only the Orient brings
To students of occult lore!
Shall I stand 'neath thy palms once more
While the radiant sun doth set
Behind temple and minaret,
Where the throbbing tom-toms beat
And the patter of naked feet
On the glowing, golden sand
Tells that a pilgrim band
Answers the call to prayer?
Shall I ever go back over there,
To the heart of mother of sons?
Mother of Warrior Sons!

I salute thee and say "Good-bye"
But I know that after I die
I shall visit thy shores again
When then [sic] cruel cycle of pain
Which Reincarnation sends,
Shatters the fragments or bends
The wheel that is circling through space,
Then shall I see thy face,
And give thee my real salaam,
With Shiva, Krishna and Brahm!
Farewell, Mother of sons!

    "OM-TAT, SAT-OM"

(*Times,* 13 May 1918, 19.)

The initials after Sir Francis' name refer to his status as Knight Commander of the Order of the Indian Empire and Knight Commander of the Order of the Star of India. Although the poem is not directly related to a local serviceman's war experience, it is a reminder that c. 1914 many local people were connected to the British Raj in various ways. (See John Bosher's works in my bibliography.)

Somewhere in France

Somewhere in France, dear comrade, you are lying
Beneath a wooden cross, which seems to rise
Out of an anguished soil whose fevered crying
Calls out on God, in pain of sacrifice.

Somewhere in France! My soul goes forth to greet you.
You are not dead! But only sleep, I know
And on the other side, I hope to meet you,
Dear gallant boy, I loved and cherished so.

(*Times,* 11 August 1918, 17)

The phrase "somewhere in France" was used by military authorities to indicate the addresses of servicemen, especially when a precise location might give away military plans.

A Siberian Impression
Written at Russian Island, Vladivostok, Siberia

Across the ice I hear the sound of marching feet
And stirring martial song! The air is sweet
And keenly cold! While from an azure sky
The sun shines down! I seem to hear a cry,
The soul of Russia breathing forth a prayer
For liberty from out a heart of care.
Across the ice I hear the sound of marching feet,
An ominous sound! Each pulsing rhythmic beat
Throbs thro' my heart, and speaks of War's red hell;
But a voice whispers from the silence, "All's well!"

(*Colonist,* 1 April 1919, 12)

*   *   *

The authorship of the following poems cannot be attributed definitely to Victoria men, often because the poets were anonymous or used only initials, and the editors did not indicate that the writer was a local soldier. The verses, however, were published in Victoria's periodicals, reflecting the attitudes expressed in the above works and the views which editors believed readers should have or—as I suggest—already did have. As well, they document the experience of many soldiers, including Victoria's, in the Great War.

J.A.A.

We're far away fighting for Britain and you.
And all that men can do, we're wiling to do
For the Empire upon which the sun never sets,
If you'll help us along with a few cigarettes.

Oh boys, you can bet that it seems a bit rough
In those long silent marches without "just a puff";
Waiting and watching and fighting, but yet
Not a taste or a smell of a wee cigarette.

We don't mind work and we're ready to fight,
We can do without food if the "Cap" says "All right".
But there's one thing we long for, so please don't forget
To help us by sending a small cigarette.

Nights and days in the trenches, with water knee deep,
We can do without fire and with but little sleep:
Shrapnel bursting over head from the dawn till sunset—
We will fight till we drop for a small cigarette.

We've left our home comforts, we've left our friends true.
All we ask I that you will remember us too.
Should we be charging Germans or chasing De Wet
We will ride straight to death for a small cigarette.

And if it is fate that in battle we fall,
And death hovers o'er us, we hear the last call,
We shan't fear the shadows, our hard luck forget,
If between our set teeth we've a last cigarette.

(*Colonist*, 11 July 1915, 4)

"'The bastards!' the gunner [a character in Acland's novel] shouted. 'They shot the cigarette out of my mouth. And it was the last cigarette I had . . .'."[27] Heavy smoking caused "trench cough", made worse by the constant wetness of the trenches. The description of water up to the soldiers' knees was often correct.

Anonymous

The Ballad of the B.C.B.s
[British Columbia Bantams]

The B.C.B.'s are going away
And all the men are feeling gay.
They're all going off to Germany
    To fight the Kaiser's army.

And when the boys do soon get in
To that pest-hole of thieves that's called Berlin,
They sure will raise an all-fired din
    And rout the Kaiser's army.

They'll get to Berlin some summer eve,
With hand-grenades right up their sleeve,
And say to the Boshes: "We'll get you, Steve;
    We're going to smash your army."

The boys are small—we all know that;
But the little fellows know where they're at,
And each has something under his hat
    For routing the Kaiser's army.

The B.C.B.'s the girls enthrall;
They'll get into Berlin some summer eve,
They'll grab old Bill in his golden hall,
    After they've smashed his army.

And when they come back to old B.C.
They'll be the notorious B.C.B.
And the reception they'll get will be good to see,
    For smashing the Kaiser's army.

(*The Bantam Review*, 12 August 1916, 9)

Anonymous

Somewhere in France

Often in my trench I think
    Of the poor chaps left at home,
Of the perils that surround them
    Wherever they may roam.

The train and tram collisions,
    The Juggernaut motor-bus;
Bacilli in the cow's milk,
    And zeppelins (which are "wurst").

How awful it must be at night
    To be in a feather bed
Or find for breakfast when you rise
    There's butter on your bread.

With all those shocking worries
    A man's life must be sad,
To think that I am missing them
    Makes me exceeding glad.

Now out here things are different,
    And life is fancy free.
We have no butter on our bread
    Nor cow's milk in our tea.

There are no train collisions
Or feather beds at night.
Zepps never, never trouble us,
But keep well out of sight.

All we have to worry us
Are bullets, bombs and shells,
Bully beef and biscuits,
And nasty, horrid smells.

So to the chaps in England
I send my sympathy,
And ask them for their safety
To come out here with me.

"This poem was written by one of the Royal Fusiliers just before the British advance at the Somme. It was picked up on the battlefield by one of the Northumberland Fusiliers and forward to England where it was published in all the leading papers. The copy received by the [Victoria] *Times* was handed to it by a member of the 67th Battalion who was badly wounded at the front, with the hope that it would help some of those who are suffering from cold feet to get a little warmth into their blood. The author of this poem was killed during the Somme advance." The *Times* published this poem at the height of the conscription crisis (29 November, 1917, 7). Although it was not written by a Victoria man, the newspaper's editors and many of their readers, civilian and military, probably shared its sentiments. "Zepps" were Zeppelins, German gas-filled airships which made a number of raids on the British Isles during the war.

Anonymous ("A Soldier in the Trenches")

The Raid We Made on Fritz

Oh, it is really very easy—
If you only know the way—
Not the slightest bit of danger,
And we do it every day.

There were seven in our party,
    The moon was shining bright.
As we crawled out on our stomachs
    Into "No Man's Land" that night.

I could hear the bullets whistle
    And the big shells bursting near,
Then the sergeant, crawling forward,
    Kicked me right behind the ear.

Next a shell dropped close beside me,
    Lucky thing it was a "dud",
But it left me lying gasping
    With my throat choked up with mud.

Then a "star-shell" floated upward,
    Making it as bright as day,
With the whole bunch lying on me
    Covered in the mud I lay.

Now we always have "fixed bayonets"
    When we go upon a raid;
Mine got tangled in my trousers
    And a nasty gash it made.

Once again we started forward,
    Crawling on our hands and knees,
But they kept the "star shells" going,
    And we had to lie and freeze.

Then I thought I saw a German
    And was just about to fire,
When I found it was the sergeant
    Tangled up in Fritz's wire.

Out and in we crawled and wriggled,
    Crossing trenches, holes and wire;
But they must have heard us coming,
    For their guns began to fire.

There we lay and calmly waited
  Till they emptied all their guns,
Then went back and took them with us—
  That's the way we capture Huns.

(*Times,* 24 December 1917, 17)

Anonymous

Keep Smiling

Laugh and be merry together,
  Wait for the end with a song,
Laugh and be merry, remember that sometimes
  Things are just bound to seem wrong.

Better the world with your gladness,
  Smile at the "barbed wires" of life,
Laugh and be glad that there's someone awaits you,
  P'r'haps mother, sweetheart, or wife.

Laugh just like brothers, together.
  Mirth never did one much ill.
Laugh that you've done what your country expected,
  Yes! And you're doing it still!

One peal of laughter makes many,
  Don't put a "grouse" in the way;
Laugh till the game is played right to the end,
  Laugh and just think, "To the Day!"

(*Times,* 22 October 1917, 4)

The reference to the war as a "game" is typical. The tone here is similar to that of the many civilian poems with titles such as "Stick It" and "Carry On" which appeared in Victoria's newspapers. The author was said to be a British prisoner of war at Doeberitz, near Berlin, where in fact conditions for prisoners were grim, because the Germans "notoriously failed to even provide them with the bare necessities of life".[28]

Anonymous

The Little Wet Home in the Trench

In my little wet home in the trench,
That's the place where we fight with the French,
The Germans all know
So we have to keep low
In my little wet home in the trench.
There's no one to visit us there.
For the place is all muddy and bare.
But I've got one friend I can trust till the end
In my little wet home in the trench.

In my little wet home in the trench
My rifle's my only defence;
If that should refuse
Then I might lose
My little wet home in the trench.
But still I should never say die,
For my comrades they always stand by
And the shots they come swift, so none of us shift
From our little wet home in the trench.

In my little wet home in the trench
When I'm in it it makes me feel dense:
But still I don't heed
When I sit down to feed
In my little wet home in the trench.
When the guns are all booming around
And the shells are ploughing the ground,
With shells dropping near, I never will fear
In my little wet home in the trench.

A sniper sat up in a trench.
I saw he was sniping at me.
I fired a shot,
And it was cold pot,
From my little wet home in the trench.

As the "Huns" they come dashing along,
The lads all strike into a song
And the Germans all know
That the lads will not go
From their little wet home in the trench.

Old England a victory will win
You'll see when the moments begin.
The Germans will go
With their heads hanging low
From their little wet home in the trench.

If only the war was to cease
At the sound of the little word "Peace"
With a fast beating heart
I would wilingly part
With my little wet home in the trench.

"Received by Miss J. Gilchrist of this city, from a friend who left Victoria with the 30th Overseas Battalion. The author is unkown" (*Colonist,* 1 October 1915, 5). Note the rare reference to the camaraderie of the trenches and the awareness that the Germans also are wet and miserable. The poem is a parody of "My Little Grey Home In The West", written 1911 by D. Eardley-Wilmot:

When the golden sun sinks in the hills
  And the toil of a long day is o'er
Though the road may be long, in the lilt of a song
  I forget I was weary before.
Far ahead, where the blue shadows fall
  I shall come to contentment and rest
And the toils of the day will be all charmed away
  In my little grey home of the west . . .

Anonymous

"The following was sent to 'Lounger' by a man in the trenches 'Somewhere in France', when he heard that Alberta had voted 'dry'."

I suppose we're a lot of heathens,
    Don't live on the angel plan,
But we're sticking it here in the trenches,
    And doing the best we can.

While preachers over in Canada
    Who rave about Kingdom Come
Ai'nt pleased with our ability
    And are wanting to stop our rum.

Water, they say, would be better
    Water: Great Scott! Out here
We're up to our knees in water
    Do they think we are standing in beer?

So, it sounds all right from a pulpit
    When you sit in a cushioned pew
But try four days in the trenches
    And see how water will do.

They haven't the heart to say "thank you"
    For fighting in their behalf.
Perhaps they object to our joking.
    Perhaps it's a fault to laugh.

Some these coffee-faced blighters
    I think must be German-bred.
It's time they called in a doctor
    For it's water they have in the head.

(*The Week,* 23 October 1915, 4)

Ernest M. Taylor, private in the First Canadian Mounted Rifles, wrote in March 1916: "There are quite a lot of hypocrites in Canada who would like to do away with the soldiers' rum ration. I should like to see them out here. I think they would alter their views considerably . . . . ."[29] As for the quality of the water supplied, most soldiers thought it tasted like gasoline—not surprisingly, since it often arrived in petrol cans. [Fig.II.6.3] On the other hand, perhaps the prohibitionists had a point. In one attack at Vimy Ridge, Pierre

Berton wrote that most of the Canadians "were slightly tipsy on the strong army rum and some were roaring drunk . . .".[30] During one attack, James Pedley noticed that "the boys had had too much rum: so that they dashed away at the first gun-fire and ran right into it [their own barrage]."[31] Will Bird also confirms the view that alcohol could be abused at the front. He reports that some soldiers got drunk on the morning rum ration. "Too much rum!" he concludes when soldiers—including officers—became careless and exposed themselves to German sniper fire.[32]

The soldier-poet, Leonard McLeod Gould, editor of *The Week,* contributed "Lounger" regularly to that periodical.

W.F.

The Draftee

I used to rise at half past eight,
    And sometimes even nine;
But now I tumble out at five
    Alert, and glad to be alive;
The marvel is that I survive;
    But, gee! I'm feeling fine!

The chicken broth I scorned at home
    I've traded for a stew
Of greasy mien and dimpled isles
    (We have to wait in serried files)

An eager crowd of reconciles,
    And hold our platters new).
The ivory ball I've traded for
    Another made of lead.

I'm reading up velocities
    And studying the errant breeze
(And stifling many a wayward sneeze)
    Without a bit of dread.

I used to think my pretty Jane
    Would give me sure the sack;
Instead she's kinder than of yore.
    Last night she waited by the door
And said at parting" Just one more
    And please to hurry back."

The swelling of my foolish head
    Has traveled to my chest;
You ought to see me puff it out
    And straighten at the sergeant's shout.
'Til now I pity every lout
    That failed to pass the test.

I've never fallen out as yet
    With any of my pals
We spend our time in "falling in"
    And marching on a daily spin
Oblivious to the sergeant's grin
    (They're uppish animals.)

And thus I mean to do my bit,
    I never meant to slack.
A missive in the letter-box
    Enclosing some of Janie's locks,
Says, "Boy. I'll send you lots of socks—
    And darn 'em when you're back!"

(*Times,* 20 October 1917, 4)

When this was published, military conscription was the law of the land. It is doubtful if a soldier wrote these lines, but editors and the authorities believed the sentiment they expressed ought to be emulated. Civilians probably also wanted to believe that this mood was widespread among both volunteers and conscripts.

G.M.D.

Rolling Up From Canada

A marching song for the 48th Battalion, Canadian Expeditionary
Force, to the tune of 'John Brown's Body'.

The 48th Battalion was recruited in the West,
We're just a bunch of brothers, and we're out to our best
If you'll put us where you want us, you bet we'll do the rest,
With a hip, hip, hip hurrah!

O, fair Vancouver Island, the country of our dreams,
We've roamed along your valleys, we've fished your
mountain streams,
And we've learned to know from childhood what "British
Empire" means,
With a hip, hip, hip hurrah!

And so we've left our ranches, our cities and our mills.
We've left our rushing rivers, we've left our distant hills
To guard our sacred heritage wher'ere our Sovereign wills.
With a hip, hip, hip hurrah!

We're rolling up from Canada, the Empire needs us all,
From furthest East to furthest West we've heard the
bugle's call.
We're out to rescue Belgium and make the tyrants fall,
With a hip, hip, hip hurrah!

Our comrades in the trenches are fighting side by side.
We're coming up to help you, lads, from distant lands
and wide.
We'll strengthen you to conquer and avenge the boys that
died,
With a hip, hip, hip hurrah!

Then throw your shoulders back boys for joy and pride
of race,
Hold you heads a little higher, with a ringing, swinging pace.

> *For it's up to us to show them when we get them face to face.*
> *With a hip, hip, hip hurrah!*
>
> *So roll up, old Victoria, we're needing more and more*
> *The kind of men who live along Vancouver Island's shore.*
> *Don't let them say we hesitate in coming to the fore.*
> *Hurrah! God Save the King!*

(*Colonist,* 28 March 1915, 4)

The 48th Battalion consisted in part of men from the 50th Gordon Highlanders and the 88th Victoria Fusiliers. The poet's early enthusiasm was typical. His patriotism, which was founded on "pride of race", included Canada as part of the British Empire. Quebeckers and immigrant farmers were conscious of this Anglo-Canadian identification with Britain, for which they felt no connection or loyalty and hence resisted conscription.

R.H. Parkinson

Goodbye B.C.

> *Farewell to you beautiful land of the West,*
> *We leave you, yet love you, forever the best.*
> *With sorrow we leave and yet eagerly go*
> *To fight till we finish Britannia's foe.*
> *Through hardships and trials and through the great fray,*
> *Your honor shall guide us, your love be our stay,*
> *And ever the thought that we represent you*
> *Shall nerve us and cheer us whatever we do.*
> *Ho! Land of high mountain and beautiful vale*
> *You gave us a spirit that never can fail;*
> *You've charmed us in peace and will aid us to dare,*
> *With coolness, the dangers our foemen prepare.*
> *Behind us we're leaving our children and wives,*
> *The homes we have built, the joy of our lives;*
> *Well knowing you'll keep them as safe as can be*
> *Enshrined in the heart of our Homeland, B.C.*
> *We've crossed the great Rockies and now on the plain*
> *Already we're longing to see once again*

The mountains and valleys, the forest and coast,
The beauties that make you fair Canada's boast;
But onward we travel determined to win
Through hosts of the Germans a way to Berlin,
And once we have done it and broken right through,
We'll come back in triumph to home and to you.

(*Colonist,* 12 June 1915, 4)

The *Colonist's* editors and their readers heartily approved of the rhetorical language ("foemen", "the fray"), the traditional values ("honor") and the imperial patriotism ("Britannia") of this poem. Of course, the love of British Columbia and Canada as the "Homeland" was less common but also appealing.

Edward John Rashleigh

Are You the Guy?

Are you the guy that walks in the street
With a crease down your pants, so trim and so neat,
And you smile at every girl you meet?
Are you?

Are you the guy that stands on the curb
And waits, as the beat of the drum is heard?
And you say, "What a fine lot of fellows! My word!"
Are you?"

Are you the guy that's seen at the dance,
Dressed in "civvies"—won't take the chance
To prove you're a man, as the others have done,
And get into khaki and shoulder a gun?
Are you?

Are you the guy that goes to the wharf
To give a farewell to a bunch that is off?
You've got a good job, it's easy and soft,
And you have only time for tennis and golf?
Are you?

Are you the guy that I've spoken about?
Then don't let it be any more.
Join up with the colors and serve our King.
Then cheers for you as well will ring,
    And you'll be a piker no more.

(*Bantam Review,* 12 August 1916, 8)

Edward John Rashleigh stood at five feet and three-quarter inches. The "slacker" was a popular theme in civilian poetry as well: see the anonymous "Slacker's Prayer" in the *Colonist* (5 August 1914, 4) in which a man who won't enlist suggests that "the women go."

By 1916, it was apparent that even British-"stock" Canadians in the Maritimes and eastern Ontario were as slow to enlist as were prairie farmers, many Francophones and organized laborers. Under the Military Service Act of 1917, all male British subjects in Canada between the ages of 20 and 45 were liable for military service. Four hundred thousand were registered, of whom 379,629 requested, and 222,364 were granted exemption. By November 1918, the Military Service Act had provided only 83,355 men and only 47,509 went overseas.[33] Conscription had little military impact on the war's outcome.[34]

*   *   *

The following verses were written by men not directly connected with Victoria, but whose poetry expressed attitudes common to local servicemen and their families. Their poems were published, mainly in Victoria, for that reason.

Walter B. Ford

The Siberians Will Stick

They tell us the war is over: that the bloody Hun is
    licked;
That we're due to get our ticket; that our trip across is
    nicked;

*They tell us our driling's useless—that we'll never fire a
    shot,*
While they hold the Bolsheviki just a gentle, harmless lot.
*So they want us home for Christmas and they're burning
    up the wires,*
*With their pleading and petitions; 'stead of burning the
    home fires;*
While the Kaiser in his castle, just across the Holland line
Wirelesses the Bolsheviki, "Ach my boys you're doing fine!"

While the politicians juggle over sending us across
*Mad with blood and loot and slaughter, Bolshevism wins
    the toss;*
*While the folks at home are pleasing for us back with
    them once more,*
*Russian homes are being broken, day by day and score
    by score.*
*"Over there" is now in Russia but its meaning's just the
    same,*
*And although home looks mighty welcome, we signed up
    to play the game,*
*Just as long as there's a Kaiser just across the Dutch
    frontier,*
Wirelessing the Bosheviki as he sips his German beer.

*Now and then a weak-kneed quitter, freedom by desertion
    seeks,*
But the line is holding steady, yellow only shows in streaks;
And we'll smite the Bolsheviki if they give us half a chance,

*And we'll scrap them just as gamely as the other boys in
    France,*
For the war will not be over 'till the Russian slate is clean,
*And the Kaiser on the Bolsheviki crutch no more can
    lean;*
*And no more he'll tune his wireless just across the
    Holland line,*
*With the Bolsheviki end grounded and a watch upon the
    Rhine.*

(*Colonist,* 12 December 1918, 4)

"Playing the game" was still a favorite metaphor with soldiers. "Over There" was a song written by George M. Cohan in 1917 and especially popular with American servicemen.

Clearly, hatred and suspicion of Germany prevailed after the armistice. The *Toronto Globe*, however, did not approve of the Siberian mission. On the other hand, the *Colonist* did, for this appeared on the newspaper's editorial page. Emperor William II of Germany had abdicated and taken refuge in Holland. The mistaken association of the Kaiser with Lenin's Bolsheviks arose from the fact that the German government in 1917 had provided Lenin with passage across Germany from his exile in Switzerland to Russia in the not unfounded hope that he and his colleagues would foment unrest there.

On 21 December 1918, as they marched from the Willows Camp to their departing ship at the Outer Wharf in Victoria, some Québécois conscripts in the 259th Battalion of the Canadian Siberian Expeditionary Force mutinied. Radical members of the local working class, enraged at profiteering and conscription, may have inspired some men. The bad weather described by the soldier-poet Shepherd and the outbreak of Spanish influenza did not help the situation. Fixed bayonets encouraged the men to board their ship.[35]

John Hooper

The Charge of the Canadians at Vimy Ridge

"Canadians, charge!" Not one of them shrank,
As their sharp full cheer from rank on rank
Rose joyously with a wiling breath,—
Rose as a greeting hail to death.
    "Forward, the Canadians,—across the bridge,—
    Forward, the Canadians, take Vimy Ridge."
    Charged well our boys each brave as his fellow,
In their faded coats of khaki yellow.
        Thro' barricade with glist'ning steel,
    O'er rifle pit and rampart real,

Crashing thro' shell-hole and glen—
Up into the Germans' den.

With bayonet and bomb they smashed their way,
And hundreds of Prussians fell that day.
Now, the wild cries of the Hunnish crew,
Now the cheering of the Canadians, too.
  "Hark—the guns—
    Thank God, the guns."
  "Action front!" the command was given,—
With hissing shell and shrapnel riven;—
The Germans broke and fled;
No one stayed but their dead;
    With curses and shrieks and cries—
    (Above us the fading skies)—
    Horses and cannon and men
    Tumbled back thro' the shudd'ring glen.

Over the dead now, year following year
(They stir not again, they raise no cheer),
As over their graves the brown leaves fall;
The whip-poor-will chants his spectre-call.
The glory of the Canadians shall never cease
Thro' time,—or even thro' the light of peace;
The glory of that charge is resounding still—
The charge of the Canadians at Vimy Hill.

(Times, 24 October, 1917, 8)

Although John Hooper was not associated with Victoria, his verses on Vimy Ridge have been included here because their appearance in the *Times* is unusual. He had been at the Royal School of Gunnery and was N.C. Officer with the N.W Field Force. In 1917 he lived in Winnipeg and was editor of the *British American Lumberman.* His poem carries echoes of Alfred Tennyson's "Charge of the Light Brigade".

*   *   *

Notes to THE SOLDIERS' POEMS

1   Quoted in Ormsby, *British Columbia*, 395-6.

2   Pedley, *Only This,* 126.

3   Canadian War Records Office. *Canada in Khaki,* Vol. I, 165.

4   Cook, *At the Sharp End*, 290.

5   Bird, *Ghosts Have Warm Hands,* 29, 30-31.

6   Service, "Rhymes of a Red Cross Man", *Collected Poems* (London: Unwin, 1915), 22.

7   Service, "Rhymes of a Red Cross Man*",* *Collected Poems* (London, Benn, 1960, 75.

8   Barris, *Victory at Vimy,* 134.

9   Cook, *At the Sharp End,* 319.

10   John Brophy and Eric Partridge, *Songs and Slang of the British Soldier: 1914-1918* (London: E. Partridge at the Scholaritis Press, 1930), 206.

11   See John Horne and Alan Kramer, *German Atrocities, 1914: A History of Denial* (New Haven: Yale University Press, 2001).

12   "Resthaven Convalescent Home is all That Name Implies", *Colonist,* 17 June 1917, 17.

13   Pedley, *Only This,* 70.

14   Acland, *All Else is Folly,* 21.

15 W.C. Millar, *From Thunder Bay through Ypres with the Fighting 52nd* (1918 [?]), 62.

16 David Mackenzie, ed., *Canada and the First World War. Essays in Honour of Robert Craig Brown* (Toronto: University of Toronto Press, 2005), 50.

17 Quoted in Goodspeed, *The Road Past Vimy*, 73.

18 Pedley, *Only This*, 230.

19 Barris, *Victory at Vimy*, 227.

20 Bird, *Ghosts have Warm Hands*, 85.

21 Service, *Rhymes* (London, Unwin, 75).

22 Morton and Granatstein, *Marching to Armageddon,* 58.

23 Service, *Rhymes* (London, Unwin), 75,

24 Acland, *All Else is Folly*, 14 and 19.

25 Miller, *Our Glory and Our Grief*, 202.

26 Radley, *We Lead. Others Follow,* 372.

27 Acland, *All Else is Folly*, 283.

28 Michael Moynihan, ed., *Black Bread and Barbed Wire. Prisoners in the First World War* (London: Leo Cooper, 1978), xv. See also Desmond Morton, *Silent Battle: Canadian Prisoners of War in Germany, 1914-1919,* (Toronto: Lester, 1992).

29 Quoted in Granatstein, *Battle Lines*, 132.

30 Berton, *Vimy,* 19.

31 Pedley, *Only This,* 164.

32 Bird, *Ghosts Have Warm Hands*, 17, and 80-81.

33 Goodspeed, *The Road Past Vimy*, 135.

34 Mackenzie, ed., *Canada and the First World War*, 62.

35 Isitt, "Mutiny from Victoria to Vladivostok, *Canadian Historical Review*, 223-264, and *From Victoria to Vladivostok: Canada's Siberian Expedition, 1917-19.*

CHAPTER IV

THE SOLDIERS' LIVES

Perhaps "Lives" is too grand a title here, because complete biographies of Victoria's soldier-poets are difficult to compile. There are, for example, cases of soldiers with the same name—even for Victoria recruits. Some careers are hard to trace because volunteers traveled directly to Valcartier or even to England in order to enlist. The following information is what was available to me at the time of publication.

ANDREW, B. De M.:

Described by the *Colonist* in 1914 as "a Victorian", he was enrolled in the 88th Regiment (Victoria Fusiliers) which had been formed on 3 September 1912. The 88th was placed on active service on 10 August 1914 for local protective duty and eventually contributed to the "Fighting" Seventh Battalion of the Canadian Expeditionary Force. Soldier-poets Robert Valentine Harvey and Edwin Freeman (see below) were also members of the 88th Regiment, the military unit which was probably most representative of Victoria's English element. This man may have been the

"Bertram Andrew", a twenty-four-year-old surveyor born in Hong Kong, who enlisted in Victoria in November 1914.

ARMSTRONG, Charles Leland:

Born 1884 in London, Ontario, he was educated there, at Mount Allison University, in New Brunswick, and at Harvard University. He worked as a journalist for the Halifax *Herald,* St. John *Telegraph,* Montreal *Gazette,* New York *Herald,* Boston *Herald,* Toronto *News,* Winnipeg *Telegram,* Manitoba *Free Press,* Vancouver *News-Advertiser* and, ultimately, the Victoria *Colonist.* In 1910, he married Jessie Agnes McKilligan. They lived on Richmond Avenue and had one son. (See "When I Kick In".)

Charles Armstrong was by far the most prolific (or at least most published) of all Victoria's soldier-poets. His first work appears in the *Colonist* on 12 December 1909—"For Another Year", in praise of BC's oldest miner. His subject matter was wide-ranging. For example, on 27 November 1910 in that newspaper's supplement, he eulogized those who perish at sea. Quasi-religious uplift was the theme of another poem published by the *Colonist* on 4 December 1910. "The Old Fort Bell" (*Colonist,* 11 December 1910) praised an essential feature of the long dismantled Fort Victoria. His "daily grind" for this newspaper was amusingly described in "The Copyhack's Christmas" (Supplement, 25 December 1910). "'Twas the Day after Christmas" parodied the already well-known poem (*Colonist,* 28 December 1910). Obviously, he was given to humorous verse, but showed little of the imperial patriotism that others expressed.

Armstrong had been on the editorial staff of the *Colonist* for several years when he enlisted in October 1915 as a private in the 67th Battalion, the Western Scots. He studied and passed the required officer's tests at the Royal School of Instruction at Work Point in Victoria and served as a sergeant in the 67th Battalion until 21 December 1915, when he was granted a commission in that unit. The *Colonist* continued to publish his poems, as did the *Western Scot* (of which he was editor). In France he contributed poetry to *Canada in Khaki* (1917), as well as a short story, and on November 18, 1916, his article on the experiences of Western Scots in France appeared in the Victoria newspaper. He spent six months in France before returning home in May 1917 on convalescent leave, suffering from cardiac problems (*Colonist,* 3 May 1917, 5). He was offered the post of Publicity Commissioner for the Vancouver Island Development Association, but instead became Publicity Commissioner for Victoria. In August 1918, he resigned and went to Chicago for advertising work. He died in 1926.

BEALE, William Joseph:

The 1911 census lists him as 47 years old in that year and living on Burdett Avenue in Victoria. Later identified as a Lieutenant-Colonel and living in 1914 at Cadboro Bay, a Victoria suburb, he submitted his "Lay of Liège" to the *Colonist,* which published it on 20 September 1914. In 1912, as Major Beale, he had assisted in the founding of the 88th Regiment to which he was appointed Adjutant. The *Times* noted that he was "formerly of a Norfolk Regiment".

BREWTON, James H.:

Identified only as "a returned soldier", living in Victoria in 1919, he published his "To General Sir Arthur W. Currie", in the *Colonist* in that year. Nothing else is known about him.

CLARKE, Harry W.:

Clarke was born in 1886. In August 1914, the nominal rolls of the 88th Regiment include H.W. Clarke as "Hospital Sergeant" on its staff. According to the 1915 Victoria Directory, he was a civil engineer, living on Mitchell Street in Oak Bay, a Victoria suburb. By 1916, he was a private with No. 1 Field Ambulance of the British Expeditionary Force. Twice in May 1916 and once in August of that year, he sent letters describing his work in the British Ambulance Corps to the *Colonist* which printed them. His submission, published on 25 May 1916, included his sentimental poem "His One Request". By 1918, he had returned to the Oak Bay address, but he died in Vancouver in 1959. Along with Lorne Ross, he is featured in the book of cartoons, *Some British Columbians 1914-1918* (Victoria: Quality Press, 1921).

CONNON, A.A. (Alexander Anderson):

Born in Scotland, Connon was twenty-nine years old when he enlisted at Victoria in September 1915. A law student, he joined the 50th Gordon Highlanders and trained at the Willows Camp where the protagonist of his poem, "The Survivor", claimed to have withstood the epidemic of mumps sweeping the base in 1916. In 1920 he married Grace Christinsen. He died in Vancouver in 1976.

In 1913, local residents of Scottish background, believing that the 88th Regiment was mainly for those of English heritage, inspired the formation of the 50th Regiment (Gordon Highlanders). The authorization came from Ottawa on 4 September 1913; Arthur Currie was appointed commander on 25 October 1913, with Major Lorne Ross (see below) as second in command (26 October 1913).

At the Caledonia Club dinner at the Empress Hotel on 2 December 1913, Lieutenant-Colonel Currie received a toast to the Gordons who, on Christmas Day that year, held a turkey shoot. In 1914, they made up part of the 16th Battalion (Canadian Scottish) and later fought at Ypres, the Somme, Vimy Ridge and Passchendaele.

FORD, Walter Bedient:

Born in Toronto in 1879, he was married, and had worked and lived in New York State as a journalist before he joined the Canadian army on 7 August 1918, in London, Ontario. By December 1918 he was at the Willows Camp, which was the headquarters for the 259th Battalion, part of the Canadian Expeditionary Force, destined for Siberia (one of two battalions,; the other was the 260th). On 21 December 1918, a group of these men mutinied as they were about to embark from Victoria, Obviously, Ford was not one of these. In fact, with the approval of his military superiors, he reported for the Victoria *Colonist* while in Siberia. (D.B. Shepherd, who objected to Victoria's rainfall, was also a member of the 259th: see below.)

FREEMAN, Edwin:

Born in England, he was thirty years old in 1914 and a private with the 88th Regiment, later with the "Fighting" Seventh Battalion. The latter was the First British Columbia Regiment, termed "salmon skinners and timber busters" by an officer from another unit. He left with them on 28 August 1914, saw action at Ypres 1915, including the first gas attack of the war, and was wounded.

In 1931 he married Emmie Harrison in Victoria, and may be the "Edwin Freeman" who lived to be 100 years old in that city.

The Seventh Canadian Infantry Battalion was organized at Valcartier on 2 September 1914 and was composed of recruits from British Columbia (i.e., including the 88th Regiment). The battalion, commanded by Lieutenant-Colonel W.H. McHarg, left Québec on 25 September 1914 aboard the VIRGINIAN, disembarking in England on 14 October. In February, 1915, they became part of the First Canadian Division, 2nd Canadian Infantry Brigade. The Seventh Battalion, which supported a fife and drum band, published the first number of *The Listening Post* on 10 August 1915. Commanded by Victor Odlum of Victoria, they were adept at raids on the enemy and also distinguished themselves in the Battle of Amiens in 1918, although Freeman was not with them at that time because by 1917 he was recuperating in Resthaven Hospital at Sidney. The 1918 Directory for Victoria has an "Edw. D. Freeman" resident on Amphion Street in Oak Bay.

I have used the first name "Edwin" although on 30 June 1915 (5) the *Colonist* reported that "Edward" Freeman was a casualty of a gas attack. On Freeman's attestation paper, on which Robert Harvey of Victoria was a witness in Valcartier, Freeman signed the document "Edwin".

GOULD, Leonard McLeod:

Born 1878 in England, he took a B.A. at Cambridge and served in the Rifle Corps there. By 1908, he was editor of Victoria's *The Week* and wrote a column "The Lounger" in that journal. He lived in the Strand Hotel. Unmarried, he enlisted at Work Point, Esquimalt, in 1915, joining the 102nd Battalion (many of whom came from northern B.C.) which became part of the Fourth Division. The 102nd attacked Regina Trench during the Battle of the Somme in October 1916. Promoted to Sergeant-Major, he won the Croix de Guerre for courage at Passchendaele. Despite his poor eyesight, which caused him "difficulties [which] he so gallantly overcame in the bewildering darkness of the trenches with their shell-torn duckboards" (*Colonist*, 22 July 1919, 5), he also earned the Meritorious Service Medal.

While in France, he sent an acorn back to Victoria, which, planted north of Fountain Lake in Beacon Hill Park, grew into a flourishing oak.

After returning to Victoria in June 1919, he wrote *From B.C. to Baisieux. Being the Narrative History of the 102nd Canadian Infantry Battalion* (Victoria: Cusack, 1919). Every chapter of this book includes a poem, typical of many such postwar histories. By 1920 he was editor of *The Islander,* a weekly supplement to the *Colonist.* He died in Vancouver in 1928.

HALLEY, Kenneth George:

Born 1879 in Scotland, Halley was a resident of Ganges, on Salt Spring Island, north of Victoria. In 1905 he married Jessie Stirling Brown in Victoria. A civil engineer, he had served with the 50th Gordon Highlanders. On 1 October 1915, he enlisted in Vancouver with the part of the 11th Canadian Mounted Rifles (many of whom were from that city). In April 1916, he transferred to the 1st Canadian Pioneer Battalion, which was converted to a Railway Troop in 1917. By 1920, "K.G. Halley" was a clerk, residing in Oak Bay, Victoria. He died in Vancouver in 1955.

HARVEY, Robert Valentine:

Born 1876 in Britain, he took an M.A. at Cambridge. In Vancouver, he was Headmaster of Queen's School but in 1908 moved his school to Victoria, amalgamating it with the new University School for Boys on Richmond Road where he became Warden. In 1912 he was a member of the "executive committee" formed to oversee the creation of the 88th Regiment which sent volunteers to Valcartier in 1914. There Harvey formally enlisted on 23 September 1914. Eventually he became a Captain, in the "Fighting" Seventh Battalion. He was wounded in action in the Battle of Langemarck, First Battle of Ypres. Taken captive, he was sent to a prisoner of war camp at Kassel in Germany where he died on 28 April 1915.

On its front page (1 May 1915), the *Colonist* carried a photograph of Harvey in uniform carrying a sword and wearing a large busby (a tall bearskin cap). At a memorial service held for him at University School in 1915, Rev. W.W. Bolton eulogized him as "a very perfect gentleman", "stern and harsh at times, . . . never overbearing." He was "the soul of honour". Harvey "gave all his money, all his time, all his thoughts" to the University School. He had donated the miniature shooting range to the school and had trained the school's cadet corps, which held "the cup for the best Cadet Corps in the Province." Bolton averred that "he died game, and with his face to the foe." No doubt Harvey was a fine soldier, but Bolton's romantic statement ignores the fact that he died in an enemy prisoner of war camp (*Colonist,* 4 May 1915, 5).

HOLLINS, Thomas A.:

Born in England in 1874, he lived with his wife, Celia Frances, on Maywood Road in Victoria. A draughtsman, he had been a bugler with Gordon Highlanders. In June 1916, he enlisted as a private and left Victoria with the 5th Field Company, Royal Canadian Engineers. Wounded in 1918, he recuperated at Bramshott Hospital, England, and later returned to Canada for further medical treatment. He died in Victoria in 1937.

JARVIS, George Victor:

Born 1894 in England, he was a chauffeur when he enlisted in Victoria, on 6 August 1915, becoming a gunner with the Fifth Regiment, Canadian Field Artillery, later with the Third Reserve Battery. He was sent to France in 1917. In 1919 he married Ethel Victoria Bridges, worked as a mechanic with the Begg Motor Company and lived on Alder Street in Victoria. He died in 1964. His daughter, Muriel Jarvis Ackinclose, published an affectionate memoir, *For the Love of George*, in 2005.

MARLING, Samuel Earl:

Born 1895 in Regina, he worked as a clerk, living on Linden Avenue, Victoria, in the home of his father, Samuel George. Having previously served with the Canadian Signal Corps, he volunteered in 1916 and was later a Signaller with the Siberian Expeditionary Force. In 1929 he married Elsie Olive Coates. He died in 1978.

MYNOTT, John:

Mynott was born in England in 1888. He had served in a militia (probably in Vancouver) and was a single laborer when he enlisted in Victoria in September 1915. By 1916 he was a private in the Western Scots. He was the contributor, perhaps also the author, of the toast to "a temperance supper". He died in Coquitlam in 1971.

PARKINSON, Richard H.

Born in England in 1870, he had lived in Kelowna. In 1905 he married Irene Margaret Haynes in Vancouver. A surveyor and civil engineer, he enlisted in Victoria on 29 May 1915 and served in the Canadian Mounted Rifles.

RASHLEIGH, Edward John:

Born in London in 1887, he emigrated to Saskatchewan in 1910. In 1916, he was single, lived in Vancouver, and worked with the "railway commissary". He enlisted in Victoria in February of that year with the British Columbia Bantams. He died in North Saanich, near Victoria, in 1969.

When war broke out in 1914, only men standing above five feet three inches in height were accepted as volunteers. The drastic loss of soldiers on the Western Front, however, compelled the authorities to accept undersized men and to form the 143rd Battalion, the British Columbia Bantams. Based at a camp in Beacon Hill Park in Victoria, the unit began recruiting in late 1915 and left for Europe in February 1917. They were absorbed into the

1st and 24th Reserve Battalions and the Canadian Railway Troops in March 1917.

REDHEAD, George:

Born in England in 1880, Redhead was living in Seattle, Washington, when he enlisted in August 1918, probably in Victoria. He was a laborer, but had served in the Royal Army Medical Corps in 1901-2 (possibly in the Boer War, where he would have heard the song "Marching to Pretoria", to the rhythm of which he suggested his verse be sung). At thirty-eight years of age, he was hardly the "boy" described by the *Colonist,* but that was the jargon of the time.

ROBERTSON, James:

Born in Scotland in 1870, Robertson had been a sawmill superintendant, was married and lived on Collison Street in Victoria, where he enlisted. He had served in the 50th Gordon Highlanders.

ROSS, Lorne:

A Montrealer, born in 1878, Ross had served as a Lieutenant with the 18th Scottish Dragoons; a Captain, with the 22nd Saskatchewan Horse; and a Major, with 29th Light Horse, Saskatchewan. He was married and lived on Faithful Street, Victoria. He described his profession as "agent". He had served in the volunteer militia—the 50th Gordon Highlanders—and led them when they left Victoria in 1914. He had formally enlisted at Valcartier in September 1914. By March 1915, he was overseas, as commanding officer of the 67th Battalion, later Lieutenant-Colonel. Slightly wounded at St. Julien, Belgium, with the 16th Canadian Scottish, he came home in April 1915, recovered and left again on 26 March 1916 with the Western Scots. He died in Victoria in 1951. [Fig.IV.1]

SCHREIBER, Charles Bryman (or Brymer):

Born in Ireland, Schreiber had served with the Northwest Mounted Police, but by 1914 he was making his home in Victoria and working with the Inland Revenue Department. He married Nina Emmeline Irving in 1909. He served as a Lieutenant, then by 1915, a Major, in the Western Scots. Wounded in 1917, he recuperated in the south of France. By July 1918, he was a member of the Permanent Conducting Staff of the C.E.F. Nina Schreiber died in 1918 and he married Annie May St. John Chisholm in 1922. In 1921, the well-known local architect, Samuel Maclure, designed a home for him on Gonzales Hill in Victoria. He died in 1937 in Sasseenos, west of Victoria.

A possible typographical error can lead to confusion here. The *Colonist* (1 August 1915, 12) gives the most thorough biography of this soldier, but spells his name "C.B. Schrieber". The poem in The *Western Scot* ("Sabaid") is attributed to "C.B. Schreiber". The website "Soldiers of the Great War" lists a Charles Bryman Schreiber, but no attestation paper can be found on line. Did the *Colonist*'s editor, not wanting to suggest that a Victoria man with such a German-sounding name was defending Canada, alter its spelling?

Fig. IV.1: Lieutenant-Colonel Lorne Ross: the cartoonist seems to have known that Ross was a poet as well as a fine soldier. He was awarded the medal of the Distinguished Service Order, and the Victory and General Service medals. (R.P. McLernan. *Some British Columbians 1914-1918.* [Victoria: Quality Press, 1921], n.p.)

SHELDON-WILLIAMS, Ralf Frederick Lardy:

Born 1875 in England, he was a farmer, had married Susan Ellen Joule in 1910, had four children, and by 1915 was living at Cowichan Station, near Duncan, north of Victoria. On 19 November of that year, the *Colonist* published on its editorial page his poem "The Passing of Bobs Badahur. November 1914." The latter was Field Marshal Frederick Sleigh Roberts (1832-1914), who had been active in India, Afghanistan and the Boer War. (The poet's interest in imperial military adventure was common in Victoria.) Sheldon-Williams enlisted in February 1916 in Victoria, becoming a Sergeant with the 10th Canadian Machine-Gun Company. By 1917, he was in France. In 1920, the Victoria City Directory lists him as a draftsman with the Harbour Marine Company. Apart from his verse printed in Victoria newspapers, he published three books and a pamphlet on his war experience. In particular, I have quoted from one of these, *Names Like Trumpets and other Poems* (privately published, 1918?) His *The Canadian Front in France and Belgium* (London: A. and C. Black, 1920) was illustrated by Inglis Sheldon-Williams (possibly a relative).

SHEPHERD, Douglas Beaumont:

Born 1896 in Windsor, Ontario, he was a single journalist, drafted under the Military Service Act of 1917. He was a Rifleman with the 259th Battalion, Canadian Rifles, part of the Siberian Expedition.

TILDESLEY, Cecil Walter

Born 1886 in England and employed as a railway engineer, Tildesley was unmarried when he enlisted at Esquimalt on 18 June 1915. He was a Gunner with the Canadian Field Artillery. He survived the war and died in Victoria in 1956.

VALLIE, J.L. (John Landon):

Born in 1893, he married Jeanne Louise Tardiff in 1929 in Vancouver where he died in 1968. Otherwise little is known about this soldier, but a Vallie family lived in Ottawa where "J.L." may have grown up with Joseph Gorman, about whom he wrote in "To Joe". By 1917, he had been wounded in action and was recuperating at the Esquimalt Military Convalescent Hospital.

VAUGHAN, Edward Manning B.:

Born in New Brunswick in 1887, he lived and worked in Alberni on Vancouver Island where his mother also lived until 1917 after which her address was in Oak Bay, Victoria. He was unmarried and a gardener. He was easily the most enthusiastic and one of the most published of Victoria's soldier-poets. On 28 November 1914 (*Times,* 4), he urged "Men of Canada, arise! . . . to guard your native land." He enlisted with the Victoria Fusiliers and was in training at the Willows by September 1915. There he marveled at "The Aeroplanes" (*Times,* 17 September 1915, 4), describing them as "the dread Valkyrie" which bomb cities "through midnight skies/ while from the stricken peoples/Mad screams of terror rise". His imperial patriotism was intense. Also while at the Willows, he wrote "Rouse Ye!", aimed at "men of British blood" (*Times*, 11 September 1915, 4). In training there he hailed "H.R.H The Duke of Connaught" promising loyalty to the Governor General who served 1911-1916 (*Times*, 16 September 1915, 4). His poem "88th Regiment, Victoria Fusiliers (To be Sung to the Air, Blue Bell)", published in the *Colonist*, 6 October 1915 (5), is filled with traditional military rhetoric: bayonets "glisten", "lifeblood" "drenches" the earth, the "foemen" will be crushed. He left Victoria with the 88th in April 1916, eventually becoming a private in the 19th Canadian Infantry Battalion Infantry, Central Ontario Regiment. He was killed in action on 9 May 1917 and is buried at the Vimy Memorial. He was "well-known to Victorians by his contributions of poetry to the Victoria press" (*Colonist*, 4 November 1917, 5).

YOUNGHUSBAND, Ralph George Napier:

Born in India in 1889, a single Roman Catholic and a farmer, he lived in Duncan. He had served in the local militia, was discharged in May 1915, and then was drafted on 11 November 1917. On 13 May 1918 (19), the *Times* printed his poem, "To India" which he "Dedicated with respect and admiration to Lieut.-Col. Sir Francis Younghusband . . .", possibly a relative. (The poem was reprinted in the *Occult Review* in its edition of May 1919. Another poem, "The Union of Souls" appeared in *The Theosophist Magazine* in 1923.) In 1918-1919, he was living in Maple Bay, north of Victoria. The *Colonist* published a romantic love poem by Younghusband, "At a Dance", on 6 November 1919 (4); "Light and laughter—and women's voices, and you not there!"

Fig.III.5: The Dream That Doesn't Always Come True".

This cartoon by Gunner Herbert Ernest McRitchie (1896-1919), C.E.F., suggests that, by 1917 at least, some Canadian soldiers were aware of the illusions which motivated their 1914 enthusiasm for military service. (Canadian War Records Office. *Canada in Khaki* (Montreal and Toronto: The Herald Press and Advertising Agency, Vol. I, 1917), 164.)

*　　*　　*

Most of these soldier-poets have long been forgotten, but their verses remain, hidden in old editions of Victoria newspapers and rarely used collections of poetry. No marble monuments or bronze statues commemorate them individually. However, as one writer noted in commenting on the few surviving veterans of that "First World War", they and their poems serve as a reminder of it, rendering it still "a presence, unfathomable and troubling in the early twenty-first century".[1] My essay may ensure that Victoria's soldier-poets and their comrades in that conflict are not forgotten. Moreover, as we try to "fathom" the "troubling" question of why they enlisted so cheerfully and what motivated them to endure an apparently unending and miserable conflict, we might examine our own twenty-first century values, political and military.

Notes to THE SOLDIERS' LIVES

1   Kate McLoughlin, Review of Peter Parker. *The Last Veteran. Harry Patch and the Legacy of War. Times Literary Supplement*, 27 November, 2009, 37.

BIBLIOGRAPHY

DOCUMENTARY SOURCES:

Canada. Army. *Nominal Rolls 88th Regiment* (Victoria Fusiliers). Archives, University of Victoria.

Canada. *Census 1911* (http://automatedgenealogy.com/census11/)

"Canadian Virtual War Memorial" (http://www.vacacc.gc.ca/remembers/sub.cfm?source=collections/virtualmem/Results)

Henderson's City of Victoria Directory for 1890 (Victoria, B.C.: Henderson Directory Co. [1890?]

Henderson's Greater Victoria City Directory and Vancouver Island Gazetteer (Victoria: Henderson Directory Co., 1908, 1915, 1918, and 1920).

"Soldiers of the First World War" (http://www.collectionscanada.gc.ca/databases/cef/index-e.html:includes attestation papers)

Taylor, Leona., and Dorothy Mindenhall. *An Index of Historical Victoria Newspapers,* Victoria's Victoria, 2007 (www.victoriasvictoria.ca).

BOOKS:

Memoirs and Diaries

Ackinclose, Muriel Jarvis. *For the Love of George. In Old Victoria and World War One* (Victoria: First Choice, 2005).

Bird, Will R. *Ghosts Have Warm Hands. A Portrait of Men at War* (Toronto: Clarke, Irwin, 1968).

Bishop, William A. *Winged Warfare* (New York: Ace, 1967).

Craig, Grace Morris. *But This is Our War* (Toronto: University of Toronto, 1981).

Dawson, Coningsby.*The Glory of the Trenches. An Interpretation* (Toronto, Gundy, 1928).

Gordon, Charles W. *Postscript to Adventure: the Autobiography of Ralph Connor* (New York: Farrar & Rinehart, c. 1938).

Jünger, *Ernst. Storm of Steel: from the Diary of a German Storm-Troop Officer on the Western Front* (London: Chatto and Windus, 1929).

Millar, W.C. *From Thunder Bay Through Ypres with the Fighting 52nd* (1918?).

Pedley, James H. *Only This. A War Retrospect* (Ottawa: Graphic, 1927).

Reid, Gordon (ed.). *Poor Bloody Murder. Personal Memoirs of the First World War* (Oakville: Mosaic, 1980).

Roy, Reginald (ed.). *The Journal of Private Fraser* (Victoria: Sono Nis, 1985).

Scott, Frederick George. *The Great War as I Saw It* (Toronto: Goodchild, 1922).

Novels

Acland, Peregrine. *All Else is Folly. A Tale of War and Passion* (Toronto: McClelland & Stewart, 1929).

Harrison, Charles Yale. *Generals Die in Bed* (New York: Burt, 1928 [1930]).

Montague, Charles E. *Disenchantment* (New York: Brentano's, 1922).

Anthologies of Poetry

Brophy, John and Eric Partridge. *The Long Trail; what the British Soldier Sang and Said in the Great War of 1914-18* (New York: London House & Maxwell, c. 1965).

Callaghan, Barry and Bruce Meyer (eds.). *We Wasn't Pals : Canadian Poetry and Prose of the First World War* (Toronto : Exile Editions, 2001).

Carman, Bliss. *Poems* (New York: Dodd, Mead, 1931).

Colombo, John Robert and Michael Richardson (eds.). *We Stand on Guard: Poems and Songs of Canadians in Battle* (Toronto: Doubleday, 1985).

Garvin, John W., ed. *Canadian Poets of the Great War* (Toronto: McClelland, Goodchild and Stewart, 1916).

Hubbard, Dominic and John Onions (eds.). *Poetry of the Great War. An Anthology* (London: Macmillan, 1986).

Kipling, Rudyard. *Collected Verse* (London: Hodder & Stoughton, 1912).

MacInnes, Tom. *In Amber Lands: Poems* (New York: Broadway, 1910).

Nichols, Robert (ed.). *Anthology of War Poetry 1914-1918* (London: Nicholson & Watson, 1943).

Osborn, E.B., ed. *The Muse in Arms. A Collection of War Poems, for the most part written in the field of action, by seamen, soldiers and flying men who are serving, or have served, in the Great War* (New York: Stokes, c. 1917).

Service, Robert. "Rhymes of a Red Cross Man". *Collected Poems* (London: Benn, 1960).

Sheldon-Williams, Ralf Frederic Lardy. *Names like Trumpets, and Other Poems* (c. 1918).

Silkin, Jon (ed.). *The Penguin Book of First World War Poetry* (London: Penguin, 1979).

Stallworthy, Jon (ed.). *The Oxford Book of War Poetry* (New York: Oxford University, 1984).

Walter, George, ed. *In Flanders Fields: Poetry of the First World War* (New York: Allen Lane, 2004).

Wetherell, J.E., ed. *The Great War in Verse and Prose* (Toronto: Wilgress, 1919).

Histories of Military Units

Bell, F. McKelvey. *The First Canadians in France. The Chronicle of a Military Hospital in the War Zone* (Toronto: McClelland, Goodchild and Stewart, 1917).

Clyne, H.R.N. and W.D.M. Sage. *Vancouver's 29th: a chronicle of the 29th in Flanders Fields* (Vancouver: Tobin's Tigers Association, 1964).

Fetherstonhaugh, R.C. *The Royal Montreal Regiment, 14th Battalion. C.E.F. 1914-1935* (Montreal: Gazette, 1927).

Flick, C.L. *A Short History of the 31st British Columbia Horse* (Victoria: Buckle, 1922).

Gould, Leonard McLeod. *From B.C. to Baisieux. Being the Narrative History of the 102nd Canadian Infantry Battalion* (Victoria: Cusack, 1919).

Lewis, Ralph. *Over the Top with the 25th [Battalion]. Chronicle of Events at Vimy Ridge and Courcellette* (Halifax: Marshall, 1918).

Macdonald, F.B. and John J. Gardiner. *The 25th Battalion. C.E.F. Nova Scotia's Famous Regiment in World War I.* (Sydney, N.S.: Chadwick, 1983).

Machum, George C. *The Story of the 64th Battalion, C.E.F. 1915-1916* (Montreal, 1956).

McLeod, John N., ed. *A Pictorial Record and Original Muster Roll 29th Battalion* (Vancouver: Latta, n.d. [1920s]).

Murray, W.W. ("The Orderly Sergeant"). *Five Nines and Whizbangs* (Ottawa: Perrault [The Legionary Library], 1937).

Radley, Kenneth. *We Lead. Others Follow. First Canadian Division 1914-1918* (St. Catharines: Vanwell, 2006).

Scudamore, T.V. *A Short History of the Seventh Battalion C.E.F.* (Vancouver, 1930).

Urquhart, Hugh MacIntyre.*The History of the 16th Battalion (The Canadian Scottish), Canadian Expeditionary Force, in the Great War 1914-1919* (Toronto: Macmillan, 1932).

Zuehlke, Mark. *Brave Battalion. The Remarkable Saga of the 16th Battalion (Canadian Scottish) in the First World War* (Mississauga: Wiley, 2008).

Historical and Literary Studies

Ashworth, Tony. *Trench Warfare, 1914-1918 : the Live and Let Live System* (London : Macmillan, 1980).

Aitken, Max. *Canada in Flanders* (Toronto: Hodder and Stoughton, 1916).

Barris, Ted. *Victory at Vimy. Canada Comes of Age, April 9-12, 1917* (Toronto: Thomas Allen, 2007).

Berton, Pierre. *Vimy* (Toronto: McClelland and Stewart, 1986).

Bindon, Kathryn M. *More than Patriotism. Canada at War 1914-1918* (Toronto: Nelson, 1979).

Bosher, John F. *Imperial Vancouver Island. Who Was Who, 1850-1950* (Xlibris, 2010)

— *Vancouver Island in the Empire* (Llumina, 2012).

Buitenhuis, Peter. *The Great War of Words. British, American, and Canadian Propaganda and Fiction, 1914-1933* (Vancouver: University of British Columbia, 1987).

Brown, Robert Craig and Ramsay Cook. *Canada. A Nation Transformed 1896-1921* (Toronto: McClelland and Stewart, 1974).

Tim Cook. *At The Sharp End. Canadians Fighting the Great War 1914-1918* (Toronto: Viking, 2007, Volume I).

Cook, Tim. *Clio's Warriors. Canadian Historians and the Writing of the World Wars* (Vancouver: University of British Columbia, 2006).

Cook, Tim. *No Place to Run. the Canadian Corps and Gas Warfare in the First World War*. Vancouver : University of British Columbia, 1999).

Eayrs, James. *In Defence of Canada. From the Great War to the Great Depression* (Toronto: University of Toronto, 1967).

Eksteins, Modris. *Rites of Spring. The Great War and the Birth of the Modern Age* (Toronto: Lester & Orpen Dennys, 1989).

Evans, Suzanne. *Mothers of Heroes. Mothers of Martyrs. World War I and the Politics of Grief* (Montreal & Kingston: McGill-Queen's University, 2007).

Fussell, Paul. *The Great War and Modern Memory* (Oxford University Press, 1975).

Goodspeed, Donald. *The Road Past Vimy. The Canadian Corps 1914-1918* (Toronto: MacMillan, 1969).

J.L. Granatstein and Norman Hillmer. *Battle Lines. Eyewitness Accounts from Canada's Military History* (Toronto: Thomas Allen, 2004).

Greenfield, Nathan M. *Baptism of Fire. The Second Battle of Ypres and the Forging of Canada, April 1915* (Toronto: Harper Collins, 2007).

Gwyn, Sandra, *Tapestry of War. A Private View of Canadians in the Great War* (Toronto: Harper Collins, 1992).

Hayes, Geoffrey, Andre Iarocci, and Mike Bechthold (eds.) *Vimy Ridge. A Canadian Reassessment* (Waterloo, Ont,: Wilfrid Laurier University, 2007).

Horne, John and Alan Kramer. *German Atrocities, 1914: A History of Denial* (New Haven: Yale University, 2001).

Hynes, Samuel. *A War Imagined. The First World War and English Culture* (London: Bodley Head, 1990).

Isitt, Benjamin. *From Victoria to Vladivostok. Canada's Siberian Expedition 1917-19* (Vancouver: University of British Columbia, 2010).

Keshen, Jeff. "The First World War in Print". *History of the Book in Canada* (Toronto: University of Toronto, 2004, Vol. 2, 1840-1918).

Keshen. Jeffrey A. *Propaganda and Censorship during Canada's Great War* (Edmonton: University of Alberta, 1996).

Mackenzie, David, ed. *Canada and the First World War. Essays in Honour of Robert Craig Brown* (Toronto: University of Toronto, 2005).

Miller, Ian Hugh Maclean. *Our Glory and Our Grief. Torontonians and the Great War* (Toronto: University of Toronto, 2002).

Morton, Desmond. *A Military History of Canada* (Edmonton: Hurtig, 1999).

Morton, Desmond. *Silent Battle : Canadian Prisoners of War in Germany, 1914-1919* (Toronto: Lester, c.1992).

Morton, Desmond. *When Your Number's Up* (Toronto: Random House, 1993).

Morton, Desmond, and J.L. Granatstein. *Marching to Armageddon. Canadians and the Great War 1914-1918* (Toronto: Lester & Orpen Dennis, 1989).

Morton, Desmond, and Glenn Wright. *Winning the Second Battle: Canadian Veterans and the Return to Civilian Life, 1915-1930* (Toronto: University of Toronto, 1987).

Ormsby, Margaret A. *British Columbia. A History* (Vancouver: Macmillan, 1958).

Read, Daphne, ed. *The Great War and Canadian Society. An Oral History* (Toronto: New Hogtown, 1978).

Rutherdale, Robert Allen. *Hometown Horizons : local responses to Canada's Great War* (Vancouver: University of British Columbia, 2004).

Sheldon-Williams, Ralf Frederic Lardy. *The Canadian Front in France and Flanders* (London: Black, 1920).

Socknat, Thomas P. *Witness against War. Pacifism in Canada 1900-1945* Toronto: University of Toronto, 1987).

Stephen, Martin. *The Price of Pity. Poetry, History and Myth in the Great War* (London: Cooper, 1996).

Swettenham, John. *Allied Intervention in Russia 1918-1919 and the Part Played by Canada* (Toronto: Ryerson, 1967).

Terraine, John. *The Smoke and the Fire: Myths and Anti-Myths of War, 1861-1945* (London: Sidgwick & Jackson), 1980.

Vance, Jonathan. *Death So Noble* (Vancouver: University of British Columbia, 1997).

Winter, Jay. *Sites of Memory, Sites of Mourning. The Great War in European Cultural History* (Cambridge University, 1995).

Winter, J.M. *The Great War and the British People* (New York: Palgrave Macmillan, 2003.

PERIODICAL ARTICLES:

Isitt, Benjamin. "Mutiny from Victoria to Vladivostok, December 1918". *Canadian Historical Review* (Vol. 87, 2006), 223-264.

Keshen, Jeffrey. "All the News That Was Fit to Print: Ernest J. Chambers and Information Control in Canada, 1914-19". *Canadian Historical Review* (Vol. 73, 1992), 315-43.

Taylor, Robert R. "The Mark of the Hun". *British Columbia History. Journal of the British Columbia Historical Federation* (Vol. 42, No. 3), 2-7.

MISCELLANEOUS PERIODICALS:

For the purposes of this study, every edition of the *The Week, The Semi-Weekly Tribune, Victoria Daily Times* and the *Victoria Daily Colonist* between 1914 and 1919 was consulted. Editions of other periodicals on the list were consulted where they were available.

The Bantam Review. (143rd Battalion, Sidney Camp, Sidney, B.C.)

The Brazier. A Regimental Journal printed at the Front by the 16th Battalion, the Canadian Scottish.

Canadian War Records Office. *Canada in Khaki*, Volumes I and II, 1917.

The Gold Stripe. A Tribute to the British Columbia Men who have been killed, crippled and wounded in the Great War. A Book of War, Peace and Reconstruction. Published for the benefit of The Amputation Club of B.C., No 2, 1919.

The Listening Post. (7th Canadian Infantry Battalion. British Expeditionary Force)

The Semi-Weekly Tribune. A Journal of Industrial and Social Reconstruction (Victoria, B.C.)

Timber Wolf. 16th Battalion, Canadian Scottish (Victoria, B.C.).

Victoria Daily Times. 75th Anniversary Supplement. 8 June 1959.

The Western Scot (67th Battalion (Western Scots). Willows Camp, Victoria, B.C. 1915-16.

The Western Scot. Commemorative Number. Yukon, Cariboo, Vancouver Island, 67th Pioneer Battalion, 4th Canadian Division. Bramshott, Hants, c. 1915-17.

INDEX

OTHER PUBLICATIONS
BY ROBERT RATCLIFFE TAYLOR

Books

The Castles of the Rhine. Recreating the Middle Ages in Modern Germany. (Waterloo, Ont.: Wilfrid Laurier University Press, 1998.)

The Great Swivel Link. Canada's Welland Canal. For The Champlain Society; University of Toronto Press, 2001. (With Dr. Roberta M. Styran)

Hohenzollern Berlin. Construction and Reconstruction (Port Credit, Ont.: P.D. Meany, 1985)

Mr. Merritt's Ditch. A Welland Canals Album. (Erin, Ont.:The Boston Mills Press/Stoddart, (With Dr. Roberta M. Styran)

The Spencer Mansion. A House, a Home, and an Art Gallery. Victoria, BC: Touchwood, 2012.

This Great National Object: Building the 19th Century Welland Canals (Kingston/Montreal: McGill-Queen's University Press, 2012) (With Dr. Roberta M. Styran)

The Welland Canals. The Growth of Mr. Merritt's Ditch. (Erin, Ont.: The Boston Mills Press, 1988 (With Dr. Roberta M. Styran and Dr. John N. Jackson)

The Welland Canals Corridor.Then and Now. (St. Catharines: Vanwell, 2004). (With Dr. Roberta M. Styran and Thies Bogner)

The Word in Stone. The Role of Architecture in the National Socialist Ideology (Berkeley: University of California Press, 1974

Articles:

"Merritton, Ontario. The Rise and Decline of an Industrial Corridor, c.1845-1939". *Scientia Canadensis. Journal of the History of Canadian Technology, Science, and Medicine.* Winter 1991, Vol. XIV, Nos. 1-2, 90-130.

"The Mark of the Hun. The Image of Germans in Popular Verse Published in Victoria, B.C. During the Great War". *British Columbia History. Journal of the British Columbia Historical Federation.* Vol. 42, no. 3, (2009) 2-7.

"A Note on Some 'Lost' Poems of Robert W. Service". *Canadian Poetry: Studies, Documents, Reviews.* No. 62 Spring/Summer 2008, 80-86.

"The Welland Canal: Creator of a Landscape". *Ontario History*, Vol. LXXII, no. 4, December 1980 (with Dr. Roberta M. Styran)